Dbt

A Practical Guide for Learning Mindfulness

(Practical Dialectical Behavior Therapy Skills to Regain Emotional Stability)

Daniel Cooper

Published By **Darby Connor**

Daniel Cooper

*Dbt: A Practical Guide for Learning Mindfulness
(Practical Dialectical Behavior Therapy Skills to
Regain Emotional Stability)*

ISBN   978-1-7779502-3-1

Legal & Disclaimer

Table Of Contents

Chapter 1: Mindfulness Skills

What is Mindfulness?

The capability to be sincerely gift, aware of in which we are and what we're doing, and no longer unduly reactive or overwhelmed via the use of what goes on round us is known as mindfulness Although everybody certainly non-public mindfulness, its miles greater effortlessly available to us even as we practice every day.

Mindfulness can be practiced thru meditation, yoga, or in truth with the aid of taking a couple of minutes every day to interest on your breath and your surroundings. Mindfulness will let you grow to be greater aware of your mind, emotions, and sensations, and learn how to receive them without judgment.

Here are a number of the benefits of mindfulness:

Increased attention and awareness

Improved emotional law

Reduced pressure and anxiety

Enhanced self-interest

Improved relationships

Increased happiness and nicely-being

There are a ton of assets on-line and at libraries in case you're interested by getting to know greater approximately mindfulness. You can also find mindfulness lessons and workshops in your network.

Here are some pointers for operating inside the course of mindfulness:

Find a quiet vicinity where you may lighten up and cognizance.

Sit or lie down in a cushty function.

Focus to your breathing at the identical time as final your eyes.

Notice the rise and fall of your breath as you inhale and exhale.

If your mind wanders, gently deliver it returned in your breath.

Continue to interest on your breath for a few minutes.

When you are finished, open your eyes and take some moments to lighten up.

Mindfulness is a easy exercising that would have a profound effect in your life. By schooling mindfulness a frequently earn to live inside the gift 2nd, be extra aware about my thoughts and feelings, and reduce stress and anxiety.

Mindfulness Meditation

The exercise of mindfulness meditation consists of being without a doubt gift within the moment without passing judgment. It is a smooth workout that might have a profound impact on your lifestyles.

The steps for training mindfulness meditation are as follows:

1. Look for a peaceful location wherein you might not be stricken.

2. Sit in a comfortable feature together with your lower back at once.

3. Shut your eyes and be aware of your respiration

4. Notice the rise and fall of your chest as you inhale and exhale.

five. If your mind stray, softly refocus them on your respiration.

6. Continue to awareness for your breath for 5-10 mins.

7. When you're finished, open your eyes and take a few moments to lighten up.

Anywhere and at any second, absolutely everyone can exercise mindfulness meditation. It is a tremendous manner to reduce pressure, and anxiety, and beautify your commonplace properly-being.

Here are a few guidelines for mindfulness meditation:

Be affected character with yourself. It takes time to learn how to consciousness in your breath.

Don't determine your self if your thoughts wanders. Simply supply it lower returned in your breath.

Make mindfulness meditation a part of your each day recurring. You gets higher at it as you workout extra.

Here are a number of the advantages of mindfulness meditation:

Reduced stress and anxiety

Improved popularity and interest

Enhanced self-reputation

Increased happiness and nicely-being

If you are interested by mastering more about mindfulness meditation, there are numerous resources to be had on-line and In libraries.

You can also discover mindfulness training and workshops in your community.

Body Scan Meditation

Body take a look at meditation is a shape of meditation that entails bringing focus on your body, from head to toe. It is a fantastic method to unwind and reduce anxiety.

Here are the stairs on a manner to do a body test meditation:

1. Look for a peaceful region wherein you cannot be anxious.

2. Take a cosy seat or lie down.

three. Put your eyes closed and inhale deeply.

4. Bring your recognition for your toes. Any emotions, collectively with tingling, warmth, or coldness, want to be noted.

5. Slowly bypass your attention up your body, from your feet on your ankles, your calves, your knees, your thighs, your hips, your stomach, your chest, your once more, your

shoulders, your neck, your face, and your head.

6. As you glide your cognizance up your body, observe any sensations. There isn't always any need to determine or trade some aspect. Simply study.

7. If your mind stray, lightly refocus them for your frame.

eight. Continue to test your frame for five-10 mins.

9. Open your eyes and take some deep breaths even as you're completed.

Here are some hints for frame check meditation:

Be affected character with your self. It takes time to learn how to consciousness on your body.

Don't decide yourself in case your thoughts wanders. Just return it for your frame.

Make frame check meditation part of your each day recurring. You gets higher at it as you exercise extra.

Here are some of the advantages of body test meditation:

Reduced pressure and anxiety

Improved interest and cognizance

Enhanced self-focus

Increased happiness and well-being

If you're interested by gaining knowledge of more about frame test meditation, there are many assets available online and in libraries. You also can discover body test meditation training and workshops on your community.

Here is a guided frame experiment meditation that you can observe:

Locate a cosy spot to take a seat down down or lie down. Put your eyes closed and inhale deeply some times. As you exhale, loosen up your body and permit flow of any tension.

Now, bring your attention for your feet. Any emotions, which includes tingling, warmth, or coldness, need to be said. There isn't any need to judge or change whatever. Simply have a take a look at.

Now, slowly pass your interest up your frame, out of your feet for your ankles, your calves, your knees, your thighs, your hips, your stomach, your chest, your lower back, your shoulders, your neck, your face, and your head. As you circulate your attention up your body, phrase any sensations.

If your mind wanders, lightly deliver it decrease again in your body. There isn't always any need to pick or punish yourself. Just be privy to your thoughts, then permit them to move.

Continue to check your frame for 5-10 minutes. Open your eyes and take a few deep breaths once you are completed. Notice the way you enjoy. Do you enjoy greater snug? More at peace?

You are unfastened to workout this meditation each time you choose. It's a exceptional way to unwind and lighten up.

Mindfulness of Thoughts and Feelings

Mindfulness of mind and feelings is a potential that let you grow to be extra privy to your thoughts and emotions and learn how to get maintain of them without judgment. It is a key factor of mindfulness-based stress bargain (MBSR) and dialectical behavior treatment (DBT).

Here are a few steps at the way to workout mindfulness of mind and feelings:

1. Locate a peaceful vicinity in that you won't be .

2. Take a cosy seat or lie down.

three. Put your eyes closed and inhale deeply some times.

four. Bring your consciousness on your thoughts and emotions. Observe your thoughts and feelings with out passing judgment.

5. If your mind wanders, gently bring it lower back for your thoughts and emotions.

6. Continue to test your thoughts and emotions for 5-10 mins.

7. When you're finished, open your eyes and take a few deep breaths.

Here are a few recommendations for mindfulness of mind and emotions:

Be affected individual with your self. It takes time to learn how to maintain in mind of your thoughts and emotions.

Don't decide your self if your mind wanders. Simply supply it decrease lower back for your thoughts and emotions.

Make mindfulness of thoughts and feelings a part of your each day ordinary. You gets higher at it as you exercising more.

Here are some of the benefits of mindfulness of thoughts and feelings:

Increased awareness of your thoughts and feelings

Reduced strain and anxiety

Enhanced self-consciousness

Increased happiness and properly-being

If you're interested in getting to know more approximately mindfulness of thoughts and feelings, there are various assets to be had on-line and in libraries. In your network, you can also find workshops and schooling on mindfulness.

Here is a guided mindfulness of thoughts and emotions meditation that you can take a look at:

Locate a comfortable spot to sit down down or lie down. Put your eyes closed and inhale deeply some instances. As you exhale, loosen up your frame and permit move of any anxiety.

Now, end up privy to your mind and feelings. Observe your mind and feelings with out passing judgment.

If your thoughts wanders, gently supply it once more for your thoughts and feelings. There isn't always any want to pick out or punish your self. Simply be aware of your emotions and thoughts at the same time as letting them go with the flow.

Continue to test your thoughts and emotions for 5-10 mins. When you're completed, open your eyes and take some deep breaths. Notice the manner you experience. Do you revel in extra relaxed? More at peace?

You can do that meditation as often as you want. It is a extremely good method to unwind and decrease anxiety.

Mindfulness of Others

Mindfulness of others is a skill that permit you to end up extra aware about the mind, emotions, and memories of others, and reply with compassion and know-how. The dialectical behavior treatment (DBT) is based totally heavily on it.

Here are a few steps at the way to exercise mindfulness of others:

1. Locate a non violent location in which you could no longer be concerned.

2. Take a comfortable seat or stand.

3. Put your eyes closed and inhale deeply.

4. Bring your cognizance to the people around you. Notice their thoughts, emotions, and testimonies.

5. If your mind wanders, lightly deliver it returned to the humans round you.

6. Continue to test the human beings spherical you for five-10 mins.

7. Open your eyes and take some deep breaths once you are finished.

Here are some suggestions for mindfulness of others:

Be affected individual with your self. It takes time to discover ways to undergo in thoughts of others.

Don't pick out your self in case your thoughts wanders. Simply deliver it returned to the humans round you.

Make mindfulness of others a part of your every day recurring. You receives better at it as you exercise greater.

Here are a number of the advantages of mindfulness of others:

Increased interest of the mind, feelings, and stories of others

Chapter 2: Interpersonal Effectiveness Skills

What is Interpersonal Effectiveness?

Interpersonal effectiveness is the capability to speak your need and dreams in a clear, respectful, and assertive way. It is a know-how that permit you to assemble and hold healthful relationships, get what you need out of lifestyles, and deal with difficult conditions.

There are 4 primary components of interpersonal effectiveness:

Expressing your want and desires: This manner having the ability to tell others what you need and want, without being aggressive or passive.

Assertively saying no: This manner having the ability to mention no to requests which you do no longer need to do, with out feeling accountable or obligated.

Making requests: This approach being capable of ask others for what you need, in a manner this is probably to get you what you want.

Negotiating: This technique being capable of compromise and find solutions that artwork for every body involved.

Interpersonal effectiveness is a capability that can be discovered out and advanced with exercising. There are many assets to be had that will help you observe those capabilities, which includes books, articles, and workshops.

Here are some hints for enhancing your interpersonal effectiveness:

Be aware about your very own needs and wants: It is essential to comprehend what you need and want earlier than you may communicate it to others.

Be respectful of others: When you're talking with others, it's far essential to be respectful in their feelings and evaluations.

Be assertive: Assertiveness is the essential thing to interpersonal effectiveness. It manner being capable of upward push up for yourself and your goals, with out being competitive or passive.

Practice makes ideal: The greater you exercise interpersonal effectiveness, the higher you turns into at it.

Interpersonal effectiveness is a valuable expertise that assist you to improve your relationships, get what you need out of lifestyles, and deal with hard situations. If you are interested by studying greater about interpersonal effectiveness, there are various belongings available that will help you.

Assertiveness

Assertiveness is the functionality to talk your want and goals in a clean, respectful, and direct way. It is a competencies that will let you get what you want out of existence, construct and keep wholesome relationships, and deal with tough situations.

Assertive people can rise up for themselves without being aggressive or passive. They can precise their thoughts and feelings in a way this is straightforward and direct, but in addition they take the other character's emotions beneath attention.

There are many blessings to being assertive. Assertive people are much more likely to get what they want out of life. They are also much more likely to have healthy relationships and be capable of cope with hard situations.

If you want to learn how to be extra assertive, there are some topics you may do. First, it's miles essential to discover your want and dreams. Once you apprehend what you need, you may begin to speak it to others in truth and respectfully. It is likewise critical to be aware about your frame language and the manner it could talk your message. Assertive humans commonly make eye touch, talk in a easy voice, and arise proper now.

Finally, it's miles vital to practice being assertive. It gets much less complicated as you exercising more. There are many assets available that will help you discover ways to be greater assertive, which includes books, articles, and workshops.

Here are a few pointers for being more assertive:

Be aware about your needs and wants: It is vital to recognize what you need and need earlier than you can speak it to others.

Be respectful of others: When you are talking with others, it's miles critical to be respectful of their emotions and evaluations.

Be direct: Assertive human beings can speak their mind and feelings a clearly and right now glaring: Assertive people receive as proper with in themselves and their functionality to get what they want.

Be prepared to say no: Assertive human beings are canon to requests that they do no longer need to do, with out feeling accountable or obligated.

Be willing to compromise: Assertive people are inclined to compromise and find out answers that artwork for everybody involved.

With exercising, assertiveness is a capability that can be located out. There are many sources available to help you take a look at those abilities, on the side of books, articles, and workshops.

Owning Your Needs

Owning your dreams is the act of acknowledging and accepting your own goals and goals. It is a way of turning into privy to what you want to sense glad, healthy, and fulfilled.

When you very non-public your goals, you're able to talk them to others in a clean and assertive way. You are also capable of set boundaries and say no to requests that don't meet your goals.

Owning your desires is an critical a part of self-care. It allows you to take duty in your very personal happiness and well-being. It additionally allows you assemble healthful relationships with others.

Here are a few hints for proudly owning your desires:

Identify your desires: The first step to proudly owning your desires is to pick out them. What do you want to experience happy, healthy, and fulfilled?

Be sincere with yourself: Once you have got recognized your wishes, be honest with your self about them. Don't try to downplay or deny your dreams.

Communicate your wishes: Once you are aware about your dreams, it's miles essential to speak them to others. This can be hard, however it's miles crucial to hold in mind that you want to have your desires met.

Set boundaries: It is likewise essential to set boundaries almost about your goals. This way announcing no to requests that do not meet your dreams. It additionally technique being inclined to walk far from relationships that don't assist your wishes.

Be affected man or woman: Owning your wishes is a device. It takes time and workout to learn how to discover, communicate, and set obstacles spherical your goals. Be affected man or woman with your self and do no longer give up.

Owning your desires is an important a part of self-care. It permits you to take duty for your happiness and properly-being. It moreover lets in you assemble healthful relationships with others.

Making Requests

Making requests is an crucial part of verbal exchange. It allows you to get what you need and want, and it moreover enables you construct relationships with others.

Here are a few tips for making requests:

Be clean about what you want: The first step to developing a request is to be clean about what you need. What are the alternative character's dreams or desires to you?

Be respectful: When you're making a request, it's far critical to be respectful of the alternative character. Remember that they will be no longer obligated to help you, so be polite and thankful after they do.

Be particular: When you're making a request, be as particular as feasible. This will assist the opposite individual understand what you need and want.

Be flexible: It is crucial to be flexible while making requests. The unique character may not be able to do precisely what you need, however they'll be capable of do a little detail else this is beneficial.

Be inclined to negotiate: If the other character isn't always capable of do precisely what you need, be inclined to barter. This way being willing to compromise and find a solution that works for every of you.

Making requests is a potential that may be found out and advanced with workout. There are many assets available that will help you test these talents, together with books, articles, and workshops.

Here are a few examples of a way to make requests in a clean, respectful, and assertive manner:

"Would you please help me with sporting the ones groceries?"

"I might admire it if you may take out the trash."

"I'm no longer satisfactory the way to do that, may additionally need to you please assist me?"

"Would you be willing to take over for me because I'm feeling overburdened?"

"I do no longer recognize if it is viable, however I really need to take a enjoy subsequent month. Would you be willing to take a look at the children?"

Making requests may be tough, however it's miles an essential talent to study. By following the ones tips, you could make requests in a manner that is probably to get you what you want, whilst moreover building superb relationships with others.

Saying No

Saying no is a effective device so as to allow you to protect it sluggish, strength, and nicely-being. It may be tough to say no, in particular if you are a humans-pleaser, however it is an crucial functionality to have a look at.

Here are some suggestions for pronouncing no in a clean, respectful, and assertive way:

Chapter 3: Emotion Regulation Skills

What is Emotion Regulation?

Emotion law is the method of managing one's emotions in a way this is adaptive and sensible. It consists of being aware of one's emotions, know-how their motives, and responding to them in a way that is suitable and useful.

Emotion regulation is a complex technique that includes several one of a kind competencies, which incorporates:

Awareness: The capability to understand and pick out out one's feelings.

Understanding: The capability to understand the reasons of 1's emotions.

Acceptance: The capability to genuinely receive one's feelings, despite the fact that they will be ugly.

Regulation: The ability to govern one's feelings in a way that is adaptive and realistic.

Everyone want in an effort to manage their emotions. It can assist us address stress, cope with tough feelings, and keep healthful relationships.

There are a number of unique techniques that can be used to decorate emotion law. Some not unusual strategies encompass:

Cognitive reappraisal: This consists of converting the manner we reflect onconsideration on a state of affairs a terrific way to alternate our emotional response. For example, if we're feeling demanding about a presentation, we might try and reframe the situation via manner of thinking about it as an possibility to share our knowledge and expertise.

Mindfulness: This involves taking note of our thoughts and feelings with out judgment. When we are conscious, we're capable of test our feelings without getting stuck up in them.

Self-soothing: This includes sporting out sports that help us to lighten up and lighten up. Some commonplace self-soothing activities encompass being attentive to track, taking a tub, or studying a ebook.

An capacity that may be learnt and advanced with workout is emotion manage. There are many assets to be had to assist us discover ways to regulate our feelings, which includes books, articles, and workshops.

Identifying Your Emotions

Identifying your feelings is step one to coping with them efficiently. It may be tough to come to be privy to your feelings, specially in case you aren't used to doing it. There are some subjects you can do to ease the way, no matter the reality that.

Pay attention for your frame: Your body regularly gives you clues about how you feel. For example, if you are feeling traumatic, you may be aware that your heart is racing or which you are sweating. If you experience sad, you may likely word which you have a lump to your throat or which you are crying.

Pay hobby to your mind: Your mind can also offer you with clues about how you're feeling. For example, in case you are feeling irritated, you may probably have mind like, "I can't receive as actual with they did that to me!" or "I'm going to get them once more!" You can assume, "I'm so nugatory," or "No one cares about me," at the same time as you are depressed.

Use a emotions wheel: A feelings wheel is a device that permit you to find out your feelings. It is a circle with wonderful emotions written throughout the outdoor. You can issue to the emotion that you feel.

Talk to a person you accept as real with: Talking to a person you do not forget can help you discover your emotions. They can listen to you and help you apprehend what you revel in.

Once you have got recognized your feelings, you could start to control them efficiently. Several tremendous strategies may be used to control feelings. Some not unusual techniques encompass:

Express your feelings: Healthily expressing your emotions will allow you to experience better. You can explicit your emotions through speakme, writing, or artwork.

Take a while for your self: Sometimes, the awesome way to govern your feelings is to make the effort for your self. This may want to mean going for a walk, being attentive to music, or reading a e-book.

Practice rest techniques: Relaxation techniques, which includes deep respiration or meditation, assist you to lighten up and lighten up.

Seek expert help: If you're suffering to control your emotions, you can want to are searching for for professional help. A therapist will let you understand your feelings and increase wholesome coping mechanisms.

Describing Your Emotions

Describing your feelings is the act of putting terms to how you are feeling. It can be useful to provide an reason behind your feelings to your self, to others, or each.

There are some subjects to maintain in thoughts while describing your emotions:

Be specific: Don't simply say you are "satisfied" or "sad." Try to be more specific, together with "I'm feeling excited" or "I'm feeling dissatisfied."

Be honest: Don't attempt to disguise your feelings. It's essential, to be sincere with yourself and with others about how you experience.

Be conscious of your intention market: If you are describing your feelings to a person else, be conscious of their feelings as properly. Don't say a few factor that would damage or dissatisfied them.

Here are a few examples of a manner to describe your feelings:

"I'm looking in advance to my tour starting day after today,"

"I'm disappointed because of the truth I did no longer get the venture I desired," someone stated.

"I'm feeling indignant because my friend have emerge as advocate to me."

"My grandmother passed away, simply so makes me unhappy."

"I'm feeling scared because of the fact I certainly have a huge take a look at the following day."

Describing your feelings can be beneficial in numerous methods. It let you to recognize your feelings better, to talk your emotions to others, and to address difficult feelings.

Here are some of the advantages of describing your emotions:

Understanding your emotions: When you describe your emotions, you're taking the time to be privy to them. This would probably help you in comprehending why you sense the manner which you are.

Communicating your feelings: When you describe your feelings to others, you are helping them to understand the way you sense. They can be more know-how and beneficial as a surrender stop result.

Coping with difficult feelings: When you describe your emotions, you are giving them a voice. This let you to experience much less on my own and more on top of things of your emotions.

If you are suffering to provide an explanation for your feelings, there are a few topics you can do:

Use a emotions wheel: A feelings wheel is a device on the way to will allow you to discover your emotions. It is a circle with exquisite emotions written throughout the outside. You can aspect to the emotion that you're feeling.

Talk to a person you trust: Talking to a person you consider permit you to recognize your feelings. They can be aware of you and allow you to recognize what you experience.

Write down your feelings: Writing down your feelings permit you to to process them and to recognize them better.

Draw your emotions: Drawing your emotions may be a useful manner to specific your self and to understand your feelings.

Describing your emotions is a capacity that can be determined out and stepped forward with practice. There are many assets available that will help you learn how to describe your emotions, such as books, articles, and workshops.

Observing Your Emotions

Observing your emotions is the act of listening to how you feel without judgment. It may be helpful to look at your feelings even as you feel satisfied, sad, irritated, or some other emotion.

Here are a few suggestions for searching at your feelings:

Pay attention to your body: Your body often offers you clues about how you're feeling. For example, if you are feeling hectic, you'll be aware that your coronary heart is racing or which you are sweating. If you revel in sad, you will probably note which you have a lump to your throat or that you are crying.

Pay interest on your mind: Your mind also can offer you with clues approximately the manner you feel. For instance, in case you are feeling irritated, you may likely have mind like "I can not trust they did that to me!" or "I'm going to get them another time!" You can think, "I'm so nugatory," or "No one cares about me," whilst you're depressed.

Label your emotions: Once you've got identified your emotions, you may label them. You may be able to higher recognise your feelings as a quit result. For example, in case you are feeling worrying, you would likely label your emotion as "tension."

Acknowledge your feelings: It is essential to acknowledge your feelings, even if they may be unpleasant. Don't attempt to forget about approximately them or push them away.

Don't decide your emotions: It is important no longer to determine your emotions numerous. Everyone feels feelings, and there may be no proper or incorrect emotion to revel in.

Be affected man or woman: It takes time and workout to discover ways to take a look at your emotions. Don't give up if you to begin with warfare with it.

Observing your feelings may be useful in numerous tactics. It can help you understand your emotions better, cope with tough emotions, and make higher alternatives.

Here are a number of the benefits of watching your feelings:

Understanding your feelings: When you look at your feelings, you take some time to be aware of them. This could probably help you in comprehending why you experience the manner that you are.

Coping with difficult feelings: When you look at your emotions, you're giving them a voice. This let you to experience less by myself and similarly on pinnacle of things of your feelings.

Making higher choices: When you have got a observe your feelings, you're able to make alternatives based mostly on common feel and cause, in choice to emotion.

If you're struggling to study your feelings, there are some matters you can do:

Use a emotions wheel: A feelings wheel is a tool in an effort to allow you to perceive your feelings. It is a circle with unique feelings written around the outside. You can aspect to the emotion that you feel.

Talk to a person you consider: Talking to someone you trust permit you to turn out to be aware of your feelings. They can listen to you and assist you to apprehend what you sense.

Write down your emotions: Writing down your feelings allow you to to way them and to apprehend them higher.

Draw your feelings: Drawing your feelings may be a useful way to specific your self and to understand your feelings.

Observing your emotions is a potential that may be learned and improved with workout. There are many resources available to help you discover ways to observe your emotions, which includes books, articles, and workshops.

Accepting Your Emotions

Accepting your emotions is the act of acknowledging and allowing yourself to sense your feelings, with out judgment. It can be tough to clearly accept your feelings, in particular in case you are used to suppressing or ignoring them. However, accepting your feelings is an vital a part of emotional health and well-being.

Here are some guidelines for accepting your feelings:

Identify your feelings: The first step to accepting your emotions is to grow to be aware of them. Pay interest to your body and your thoughts, and observe if you may select out the emotion you feel.

Label your feelings: Once you have got recognized your feelings, label them. You can be capable of higher recognize your emotions as a stop end end result. For example, if you are feeling stressful, you may possibly label your emotion as "anxiety."

Acknowledge your emotions: It is vital to well known your emotions, regardless of the reality that they are unpleasant. Don't try and push them away or forget approximately approximately them.

Don't decide your emotions: It is vital no longer to decide your feelings. Everyone feels emotions, and there may be no proper or incorrect emotion to experience.

Be affected character: It takes time and exercise to discover ways to gather your feelings. Don't give up if you to begin with conflict with it. Here are a few blessings of accepting your feelings:

Reduce pressure and tension: When you get hold of your emotions, you're no longer in search of to combat them or suppress them. Stress and tension may be lessened as a end quit end result.

Improve self-attention: When you acquire your emotions, you are getting to know yourself better. This will assist you to to apprehend your triggers and a way to deal with difficult feelings.

Build resilience: When you receive your feelings, you are studying to tolerate them. This will let you to construct resilience and deal with difficult conditions.

If you're struggling to absolutely take transport of your emotions, there are some matters you may do:

Talk to a person you receive as right with: Talking to someone you consider let you to become aware about and receive your feelings. They can pay attention to you and allow you to recognize what you experience.

Write down your feelings: Writing down your feelings allow you to to tool them and to understand them better.

Become greater conscious: The area of mindfulness consists of being in the second with out passing judgment. This let you to emerge as more aware of your emotions and to absolutely take delivery of them with out judgment.

Chapter 4: Distress Tolerance Skills

What is Distress Tolerance?

Distress tolerance is the ability to control tough feelings and situations in a healthful way. It's a ability that may be picked up and developed with paintings.

There are many extraordinary techniques to exercise misery tolerance. Some not unusual techniques encompass:

Mindfulness: The area of mindfulness includes being in the 2nd with out passing judgment. When we are conscious, we're capable of check our feelings with out getting caught up in them.

Self-soothing: Self-soothing is the act of assignment sports that help us to lighten up and relax. Some commonplace self-soothing sports sports encompass taking note of tune, taking a tub, or analyzing a ebook.

Distraction: Distraction is the act of focusing on some issue else that lets in you to take our thoughts off of our feelings. Some not unusual distractions consist of watching TV, playing video games, or going for a walk.

Acceptance: Acceptance is the act of acknowledging our feelings without judgment. When we take transport of our emotions, we are able to permit them to transport with out trying to alternate them.

Problem-solving: Problem-solving is the act of figuring out the supply of our distress and developing a plan to address it.

Distress tolerance is an important capabilities for everybody to have. It can help us to cope with strain, address tough emotions, and hold healthful relationships.

If you are struggling with distress tolerance, there are various assets available to help you. A therapist, counselor, or exquisite intellectual fitness expert is available for consultation. Online substances and facts are also to be had.

Here are some additional guidelines for distress tolerance:

Take some time for yourself: Sometimes, the great way to govern your emotions is to take some time for yourself. This have to advocate going for a walk, paying attention to song, or analyzing a ebook.

Practice relaxation strategies: Relaxation strategies, which incorporates deep breathing or meditation, allow you to to loosen up and loosen up.

Talk to someone you recollect: Talking to someone you get hold of as proper with will assist you to to way your emotions and to revel in higher.

Avoid alcohol and capsules: Alcohol and drugs can worsen your emotions and make it more hard to adjust them.

Get enough sleep: When you're nicely-rested, you're higher able to manipulate your emotions.

Eat a wholesome healthy dietweight-reduction plan: Eating a healthful weight loss program can help to enhance your mood and reduce strain.

Exercise often: Exercise is a fantastic manner to relieve pressure and decorate your mood.

Set sensible expectations: Don't assume yourself to be best. Everyone makes errors, and this is k.

Be kind to your self: Treat your self with the identical compassion and understanding which you can treat a friend.

Distress tolerance is an critical talent that assist you to to stay a happier and greater wholesome existence. By following the ones suggestions, you may learn how to control your emotions in a manner this is adaptive and useful.

Self-Soothing

Self-soothing is the practice of wearing out sports activities that help you relax out and loosen up. It is a wholesome manner to address pressure and hard feelings.

There are many one in all a type self-soothing sports activities sports that you may try. Some not unusual examples consist of:

Taking a heat bathtub or shower.

Listening to calming music.

Reading a e-book.

Spending time in nature.

Massaging your personal frame.

Drinking a cup of tea or espresso.

Yoga or meditation.

Talking to a pal or member of the family.

Doing some problem progressive, which includes portray, drawing, or writing.

Taking a snooze.

It is crucial to find out self-soothing sports sports that provide you with the consequences you want and that you revel in. When you feel pressured or beaten, attempt to interact in this type of sports that will help you lighten up and lighten up.

Here are a few extra suggestions for self-soothing:

Be affected character: It takes time to discover ways to self-soothe effectively. Don't get discouraged in case you do now not find something that works right away.

Be flexible: What works for you sooner or later might not paintings the subsequent. Be open to attempting many techniques until you find out the only that works fantastic.

Make it a addiction: The greater you exercise self-soothing, the better you will become at it. Make it a dependancy to interact in self-soothing sports activities on a everyday basis, even while you aren't feeling harassed or beaten.

Self-soothing is an important potential for all of us to have. It allow you to address stress, cope with difficult feelings, and maintain wholesome relationships. By following those pointers, you could discover ways to self-soothe successfully and live a happier and more healthy life.

Radical Acceptance

Radical popularity is the workout of accepting matters as they're, with out judgment. It is a manner of letting bypass of the need to control or trade subjects which is probably past our manage.

Radical recognition can be a difficult practice, however it could be very useful in reducing suffering. When we be given topics as they're, we aren't stopping in opposition to truth. This can result in a enjoy of peace and calm.

There are many benefits to radical recognition. Some of these blessings encompass:

Reduced suffering: When we get hold of subjects as they may be, we are not stopping toward fact. This can bring about a experience of peace and calm.

Increased self-compassion: Radical popularity can assist us to be more compassionate in the direction of ourselves. When we be given our personal flaws and errors, we are lots a great deal less in all likelihood to be difficult on ourselves.

Improved relationships: Radical popularity can assist us to have better relationships with others. When we receive others for who they're, we're less possibly to be critical or judgmental.

If you are interested in gaining knowledge of greater about radical recognition, there are various sources available. You can find out books, articles, and workshops at the priority. You can also speak to a therapist or counselor who will let you discover ways to exercising radical beauty.

Here are some tips on radical reputation:

Identify the assets you're resisting: The first step to radical recognition is to find out the things you are resisting. What are the topics on your existence that you are attempting to trade or control?

Acknowledge your resistance: Once you have identified the belongings you are resisting, widely diagnosed your resistance. Don't try and push it away or neglect approximately it.

Allow your self to revel in your emotions: When you're resisting some element, you are probably feeling some terrible emotions. Without passing judgment, allow yourself to experience those emotions.

Accept the scenario as it's far: The very last step is to simply accept the situation as it's miles. This could no longer imply that you have to find it irresistible or don't forget it. It truly technique which you are willing to permit cross of the need to exchange it.

Radical splendor is a workout that takes effort and time. However, it may be a totally useful device in decreasing struggling and living a happier and greater wholesome lifestyles.

Contingency Management

A behavioral intervention known as contingency manage (CM) makes use of incredible reinforcement to promote suitable behaviors. In CM, people are rewarded for assembly specific dreams, which includes attending remedy intervals, submitting drug-free urine samples, or finishing one-of-a-kind obligations. The rewards may be tangible, which include coins or prizes, or they'll be intangible, which incorporates praise or privileges.

CM has been confirmed to be powerful in plenty of settings, which encompass substance abuse treatment, intellectual health remedy, and education. It is specifically effective in treating substance abuse troubles, and it is been confirmed to reduce relapse prices and decorate treatment outcomes.

There are a number of splendid strategies to put into effect CM. The most common approach is to use a voucher tool. In a voucher device, humans earn vouchers for assembly their desires. These vouchers can then be redeemed for objects or offerings, together with food, apparel, or leisure.

Other tactics to CM include:

Prize reinforcement: Participants are given prizes for meeting their desires. Prizes may be some difficulty from small trinkets to high-priced gadgets.

Token financial system: Participants earn tokens for assembly their dreams. Tokens can then be redeemed for rewards, collectively with food, privileges, or sports.

Gamification: CM is made extra amusing and engaging by way of the use of the use of activity-like factors, which encompass elements, levels, and rewards.

CM is a flexible intervention that may be tailored to satisfy the goals of man or woman participants and settings. It is a promising approach to behavior alternate that has the ability to improve consequences for plenty of populations.

Here are some of the blessings of contingency manage:

Increased motivation: CM can help to growth motivation with the resource of way of providing members with a tangible incentive for meeting their desires.

Improved remedy outcomes: CM has been hooked up to beautify treatment results for an entire lot of conditions, along with substance abuse troubles and highbrow health problems.

Reduced relapse expenses: CM can help to lessen relapse fees via imparting contributors with a way to preserve their development after treatment.

Increased self-efficacy: CM can assist to growth self-efficacy via way of presenting people with first rate reinforcement for his or her efforts.

Chapter 5: Understanding Dbt

Susan has become a ordinary adolescent. She had an entire lot of buddies, became very social, and generally regarded to be smiling Susan, but, modified into handling some excessive emotional issues. She struggled with anxiety, depression, and excessive temper swings that left her feeling crushed and hopeless. She had attempted the whole thing, from medication to treatment, to get better, however nothing seemed to art work.

Susan's mother and father then suggested she strive dialectical behavior treatment (DBT). Susan changed into uncommon with DBT, but she has come to be willing to attempt some element to enjoy higher. She changed into involved and unsure of what to anticipate throughout her first consultation.

The therapist commenced through outlining the basics of DBT. It modified into a form of remedy that aimed to teach people a way to control their emotions and behaviors. The therapist explained that people with emotional problems often war with emotion law, which results in impulsive and detrimental conduct. DBT changed into created to assist humans in getting to know the way to modify their feelings to be able to make higher choices and decorate their common great of existence.

Susan modified into skeptical earlier than the whole thing. She had been to therapy earlier than and in no manner placed it especially useful. However, due to the reality the therapist endured to provide an explanation for the thoughts of DBT, Susan decided out that it modified into in assessment to some factor she had attempted in advance than. The therapist referred to DBT's 4 critical components: mindfulness, misery tolerance, emotion regulation, and interpersonal effectiveness.

Mindfulness is described because the capacity to be gift inside the second and aware about one's thoughts and emotions. Susan had generally struggled with this; she grow to be always concerned about the destiny or ruminating on the beyond. The therapist, however, taught her strategies for focusing her hobby at the winning 2nd, alongside aspect deep respiratory and body scanning.

The goal of distress tolerance emerge as to discover ways to address difficult conditions without resorting to horrific behavior. Susan had a bent to lash out at the same time as dissatisfied, however the therapist taught her coping competencies collectively with going for a stroll, paying attention to tune, or writing in a mag.

Emotion regulation is prepared learning to recognize and manipulate sturdy feelings. Susan had continuously felt as even though her feelings were out of manage, but the therapist taught her a way to understand the physical sensations that determined her emotions and the way to calm herself down.

Learning how to talk efficaciously with others and bring together top notch relationships is imperative to interpersonal effectiveness.

Susan had always struggled in social conditions, but her therapist taught her a way to say her dreams and set wholesome boundaries.

Susan labored hard on those skills over the course of severa months. It wasn't easy, and there had been times at the same time as she desired to give up. But her therapist become usually there to inspire her and maintain her heading in the right path.

Susan regularly started out out out to phrase a shift in herself. She have become plenty much less reactive to conditions that used to make her crazy. She modified into better capable of address war and talk with others. She felt more on top of factors of her emotions than they did of her.

But probable the maximum top notch alternate modified into Susan's thoughts-set toward herself. She felt like she have become making progress for the primary time in a long time. She modified into pleased with herself for all of her tough artwork, and she or he or he became positive approximately her destiny.

Susan's DBT adventure emerge as no longer constantly smooth, but it emerge as nicely properly well worth it. She obtained self assurance and vanity that she had in no manner had earlier than, and she or he discovered capabilities that she would possibly use for the relaxation of her life.

Consider giving DBT a strive if you or someone is experiencing emotional problems. It isn't always a brief recovery, but it's going to let you discover ways to manage your emotions and live a happier, extra wholesome lifestyles with dedication and hard art work.

WHAT IS DBT AND HOW DOES IT WORK?

Dialectical conduct remedy (DBT) is a quite powerful shape of remedy that combines cognitive-behavioral therapy (CBT) elements with mindfulness and popularity strategies. DBT changed into advanced in the 1980s via psychologist Marsha Linehan with the cause of treating borderline person ailment (BPD), however it has in the end been efficaciously used to deal with plenty of highbrow health troubles, which encompass substance abuse, consuming troubles, anxiety, and despair.

DBT works via manner of schooling people a manner to govern their emotions, improve their relationships, and beautify their average exceptional of life. The therapy is based totally totally at the concept of dialectics, which states that apparently contradictory thoughts can both be actual. For example, a person may love and hate someone or want to exchange at the same time as additionally resisting alternate. DBT acknowledges that the ones opposing thoughts can coexist and that people can learn how to take shipping of and art work with them in desire to looking to eliminate one or the other.

Individual remedy durations, agency therapy, and abilties education are commonly used to deliver treatment. Individual remedy training are commonly held as quickly as per week and are geared closer to assisting the person in growing capabilities for handling their emotions and conduct. The therapist assists the patron in figuring out emotional triggers, growing coping strategies, and running thru any beyond traumas or conflicts that can be contributing to their modern troubles.

Group treatment classes are usually held as quickly as every week and incorporate a small employer of oldsters which are coping with similar troubles. Individuals can percent their reviews, workout new abilties, and collect comments from the therapist and exclusive group people in a consistent surroundings. Role-playing physical games will also be utilized by the therapist to assist humans exercising interpersonal abilties along with assertiveness and conflict resolution.

DBT calls for functionality schooling, which includes analyzing 4 middle capability modules: mindfulness, distress tolerance, emotion law, and interpersonal effectiveness. Mindfulness is the workout of being honestly present in the 2d, and it is used to help humans come to be greater aware of their thoughts, emotions, and behaviors. Individuals with distress tolerance skills can tolerate and control excessive emotions without resorting to self-negative behaviors. Individuals with emotional law competencies can choose out and exchange horrible concept patterns further to manage excessive emotions. Individuals with interpersonal effectiveness skills are higher able to form healthy relationships and talk effectively with others.

DBT is a motive-orientated, installed remedy that commonly lasts 6 months to a three hundred and sixty five days. The length of treatment, alternatively, can variety depending at the person's unique wishes and goals. DBT has been confirmed to be extraordinarily powerful in treating a whole lot of highbrow health conditions, including borderline person ailment, depression, anxiety, and substance abuse.

One of DBT's key strengths is its emphasis on each popularity and trade. Individuals may additionally furthermore have horrible mind and emotions that cannot be eliminated, but the treatment teaches them the manner to manipulate those mind and emotions efficiently. This method helps people advantage more manipulate over their lives and improves their ordinary top notch of existence.

DBT also emphasizes the recovery dating most of the character and the therapist. The remedy is provided in a nonjudgmental and supportive surroundings that encourages open and honest verbal exchange. This technique makes people experience heard and understood, that is specially critical for people who've professional trauma or abuse.

DBT is a surprisingly effective form of remedy that mixes cognitive-behavioral treatment factors with mindfulness and popularity strategies. Based at the idea of dialectics, the remedy teaches human beings the manner to control their feelings, beautify their relationships, and enhance their commonplace amazing of lifestyles. DBT is a fixed up and aim-oriented treatment that has been validated to be specifically powerful in treating some of intellectual fitness situations. It usually lasts six months to a 12 months.

THE HISTORY AND EVOLUTION OF DBT

Dialectical behavior remedy (DBT) is a therapeutic method that has acquired reputation in modern day years. DBT is a form of cognitive-behavioral treatment that grow to be to begin with superior to cope with human beings stricken by borderline persona illness (BPD), but it has considering the reality that been applied to 1-of-a-kind mental health situations which incorporates eating issues, substance abuse, and post-disturbing pressure sickness (PTSD). DBT has been set up to be an effective remedy for those who conflict with emotional dysregulation, impulsivity, and interpersonal dating problems.

DBT dates yet again to the 1970s, whilst Dr. Marsha Linehan, a systematic psychologist, commenced running with individuals who were suicidal or self-harming, a number of whom had been identified with BPD. BPD emerge as considered a tough situation to cope with on the time due to the truth people with BPD often struggled with excessive emotional research, impulsive behaviors, and interpersonal problems. Dr. Linehan placed that conventional kinds of psychotherapy, at the side of psychodynamic therapy, have been vain for those people and that quite a few them were regularly hospitalized because of their signs and signs and symptoms.

Dr. Linehan believed that people affected by BPD needed greater primarily based and targeted therapy. She blended cognitive-behavioral remedy (CBT) standards, which emphasize the significance of identifying and changing terrible thoughts and behaviors, with mindfulness factors, which include being present and aware about one's thoughts and emotions with out judgment. Dr. Linehan additionally brought a dialectical aspect to the treatment, which includes balancing opposing viewpoints and locating common floor.

Individual treatment, company abilties education, cell phone coaching, and therapist consultation groups comprised the number one version of DBT, which became developed within the Nineteen Eighties. Individual remedy instructions emphasised figuring out and converting poor thoughts and behaviors, whilst agency abilties schooling instructions emphasised schooling patients sensible capabilities for managing their feelings, interpersonal relationships, and different disturbing situations. The mobile phone education component allowed patients to the touch their therapist for assist out of doors of classes, whilst the therapist session corporations supported and guided the therapists turning inside the remedy.

DBT has advanced and accelerated beyond its proper recognition on BPD over the years. DBT is now used to cope with some of intellectual fitness troubles, which includes eating problems, substance abuse, PTSD, and depression. DBT has moreover been carried out in plenty of settings, along side faculties, hospitals, and correctional facilities.

The addition of online and cell-primarily based components to DBT treatment has been one of the maximum giant dispositions. With the development of telehealth and mobile technology, therapists can now supply DBT to sufferers remotely, making the treatment greater to be had to those who might not be able to get right of entry to in-individual treatment. Videoconferencing durations with a therapist, as well as on line abilties education modules and homework assignments, are common talents of on-line DBT applications.

Another problem of DBT evolution has been the improvement of specialized variations for numerous populations. DBT, as an instance, has been tailored for children, who may also moreover face particular problems with emotional regulation and social interactions. DBT has moreover been tailor-made for human beings stricken by substance abuse troubles who also can want extra help managing cravings and warding off relapse.

Despite its evolution, DBT's center ideas remain normal. DBT stresses the significance of balancing reputation and trade, which incorporates accepting oneself and one's conditions at the same time as moreover taking walks to exchange horrible perception and behavior patterns. DBT additionally emphasizes the fee of mindfulness, which entails being present and aware of one's own mind and emotions with out judgment. DBT abilties, which incorporates distress tolerance, emotional law, and interpersonal effectiveness, are intended to help human beings in managing their emotions, dealing with pressure, and improving their relationships.

Chapter 6: The 4 Modules Of Dbt Skills Training

Teenagers are going through a length of exquisite change and project in their lives. They are often subjected to educational, social, and physical modifications that may be overwhelming. These stressful conditions can result in anxiety, overwhelming feelings, and a lack of resilience. Fortunately, for young adults who're struggling with those problems, the 4 modules of DBT abilties training may be useful.

The four modules of DBT talents schooling are supposed to help humans take a look at capabilities for dealing with difficult feelings, decreasing dangerous behaviors, and enhancing interpersonal relationships. Mindfulness, emotion law, distress tolerance, and interpersonal effectiveness are a number of the modules covered.

Mindfulness

Mindfulness is the primary module of DBT abilities education. The exercising of being aware about the prevailing second with out judgment is referred to as mindfulness. It is a powerful tool for dealing with difficult feelings, reducing pressure, and improving considerable well-being. Meditation, respiratory strategies, and aware remark are some of the sporting occasions used to train mindfulness.

Mindfulness exercise can be especially beneficial for folks that be stricken with the useful resource of tension, despair, or extraordinary highbrow fitness problems. Individuals can learn how to be extra aware about their mind, emotions, and behaviors through that specialize in the gift second and accepting it without judgment. This interest can help them pick out out styles of bad wondering and conduct and art work to alternate the ones styles over time.

Mindfulness may be especially useful for young adults who're filled with tension. Anxiety can reason people to ruminate on past sports activities or fear approximately destiny sports, vital to feelings of weigh down. Mindfulness teaches humans to cognizance at the prevailing 2nd, that may help them feel a great deal less disturbing and greater relaxed.

Teaching teenagers mindfulness abilities can help them expand a extra feel of self-consciousness, which could improve their emotional regulation. Teenagers can discover ways to find out their thoughts and emotions via the usage of practising mindfulness, that can help them control their emotions in a more healthy manner. Mindfulness can also help young adults amplify resilience with the useful resource of coaching them to interest on the winning moment and feature a more superb outlook on existence.

Emotion Regulation

Emotion regulation is the second module of DBT skills education. The method of managing and modifying extreme or hard emotions is referred to as emotion regulation. This module teaches humans the way to turn out to be aware about and label their emotions, recognize the characteristic in their emotions, and expand healthy coping techniques.

Individuals who conflict with emotional dysregulation, alongside aspect humans with borderline man or woman ailment, want in order to alter their emotions. Individuals who discover ways to alter their feelings can lessen impulsive behavior, enhance their relationships, and enhance their normal extremely good of existence.

Teenagers often revel in overwhelming feelings, that may result in impulsive behavior and poor choice-making. Emotion regulation capabilities can assist young adults manage their feelings greater efficiently, that can bring about higher preference-making and plenty much less impulsive behaviors.

Teenagers can increase a greater experience of self-consciousness through reading the way to pick out out and label their emotions. This self-reputation can help them in figuring out the triggers that reason overwhelming feelings, permitting them to interfere earlier than their feelings turn out to be too intense. Teenagers can lessen the terrible impact in their emotions on their every day lives with the aid of the use of way of growing a stronger sense of emotional regulation.

Distress Tolerance

Distress tolerance is the 0.33 module of DBT talents education. Distress tolerance is the capability to tolerate and live on distressing situations with out carrying out dangerous behaviors. This module teaches human beings a manner to address traumatic conditions in a wholesome manner by using the use of the use of using strategies which includes distraction, self-soothing, and disaster survival.

Individuals who battle with self-damage or suicidal mind need to exercise misery tolerance. Individuals can lessen their threat of self-harm or suicide by way of way of analyzing a manner to tolerate distressing conditions with out wearing out risky behaviors.

Distress tolerance can be mainly useful for teenagers who're experiencing overwhelming emotions. Teenagers with low distress tolerance can also hotel to unstable behaviors together with substance abuse or self-damage to cope with their feelings.

Teenagers can boom healthier coping mechanisms for managing distressing situations by reading distress tolerance skills. This can lessen the opportunity of challenge dangerous behaviors and boom resilience. Distress tolerance abilties can also assist teenagers in growing a more potent experience of self-efficacy, which could enhance their regular properly-being.

Interpersonal Effectiveness

Interpersonal effectiveness is the fourth DBT expertise education module. The potential to talk efficaciously with others and keep wholesome relationships is called interpersonal effectiveness. This module teaches people a way to set wholesome boundaries, explicit their wishes and dreams, and negotiate battle.

Individuals who battle with relationships, alongside facet humans with borderline man or woman ailment, require interpersonal effectiveness. Individuals can decorate their ordinary superb of life and decrease feelings of isolation and loneliness thru studying a manner to talk effectively and hold healthy relationships.

Teenagers often face interpersonal problems, collectively with peer pressure and bullying. Interpersonal effectiveness talents can assist teens in growing healthful relationships and efficaciously speakme with others.

Teenagers can reduce their chances of being in horrible relationships with the aid of way of studying the way to set limitations and unique their needs and desires in a healthful way. Interpersonal effectiveness abilities can also sell increased self-confidence, that may enhance regular properly-being and resilience.

DBT capabilities education is a terrific tool for coping with tough emotions, lowering risky behaviors, and enhancing interpersonal relationships. Mindfulness, emotion regulation, distress tolerance, and interpersonal effectiveness are the four modules of DBT skills training. Individuals can beautify their normal properly-being and decrease the terrible impact of highbrow fitness troubles via manner of manner of studying those skills.

The 4 modules of DBT abilities education can be useful for teenagers who're experiencing tension, overwhelming emotions, or a loss of resilience. Teenagers can expand greater healthy coping mechanisms, enhance their emotional law, and gain a more sense of self-efficacy and self-self assurance with the aid of the usage of gaining knowledge of mindfulness, emotion law, distress tolerance, and interpersonal effectiveness abilties. DBT abilities schooling can be an effective device for promoting young adults' highbrow health and nicely-being.

HOW DBT CAN BENEFIT TEENS WITH ANXIETY AND OVERWHELMING EMOTIONS

Sophie turned into a modern day 15-12 months-vintage girl with masses occurring in her life. She was managing the pressure of schoolwork, extracurricular sports activities, and excessive college social dynamics. She come to be additionally coping with anxiety and overwhelming emotions that seemed to pop out of nowhere. She felt like she could not control her mind and emotions, and it modified into affecting her each day life.

Sophie's parents noticed she modified into suffering extra than ordinary finally. They were involved about her mental health and decided to are trying to find help. They sought the services of a therapist who specialised in dialectical behavior remedy (DBT). DBT is a shape of remedy this is particularly useful for people who've emotional dysregulation, which includes Sophie.

Sophie modified into first of all skeptical of treatment. She had in no manner seen a therapist in advance than, and the opportunity of discussing her emotions with a stranger changed into intimidating. However, after some durations, she started to look the benefits of DBT. Here are a number of the strategies DBT assisted Sophie in dealing with her tension and overwhelming emotions:

Learning Mindfulness Skills

DBT teaches mindfulness competencies that assist human beings in very last present within the second and dealing with their emotions. Sophie discovered out to be aware of her breathing and her thoughts and feelings without judging them. She moreover observed out the way to apply her senses to ground herself while she felt demanding or overwhelmed. Sophie changed into able to lessen her anxiety and experience greater on top of things of her emotions via operating closer to those talents on a everyday foundation.

Understanding Emotional Regulation

One of the primary desires of DBT is to assist humans in records and regulating their emotions. Sophie determined out to understand diverse emotions further to the bodily sensations that accompany them. She moreover determined the manner to perceive her emotional triggers and increase coping techniques for them. Sophie have become able to talk her desires greater efficiently and avoid emotional outbursts with the useful resource of better records her feelings.

Improving Interpersonal Communication Skills

DBT additionally emphasizes the development of interpersonal skills which encompass conversation and problem-fixing. Sophie found out the manner to particular her goals and dreams in a healthful manner, further to a way to actively be aware of others. She additionally found out the way to treatment conflicts and treatment problems. Sophie turned into capable of decorate her interpersonal abilities and reduce her social anxiety with the useful resource of strengthening her relationships together together with her circle of relatives and friends.

Chapter 7: Fighting Negative Thoughts

One of Sophie's most hard stressful situations modified into dealing with terrible thoughts that regarded to spiral out of manipulate. DBT teaches human beings the way to confront and update lousy thoughts with more excessive pleasant ones. Sophie found to apprehend cognitive distortions like each-or-no longer anything wondering and catastrophizing and replace them with extra realistic thoughts. Sophie became able to reduce her anxiety and enhance her temper through using tough her negative thoughts.

Using Coping Mechanisms

Finally, DBT teaches people the manner to apply numerous coping techniques on the equal time as they're feeling crushed or stressful. Sophie decided out the manner to lessen her anxiety with the resource of the use of rest techniques which embody deep respiratory and present day muscle relaxation. She moreover located the manner to use distraction techniques to take her mind off her issues, at the facet of taking note of tune or going for a walk. By having a toolbox of coping techniques, Sophie became able to control her tension and overwhelming feelings extra successfully.

Sophie's intellectual health progressed considerably after several months of DBT. She felt more on pinnacle of factors of her feelings and changed into able to deal with her anxiety more correctly. She have end up moreover greater confident in her interpersonal abilties and felt higher prepared to cope with social situations. Sophie had been given the tools she needed to navigate the worrying conditions of youngsters and stay a happier, greater enjoyable lifestyles because of DBT.

DBT can be an powerful treatment alternative in case you or a person you recognise is suffering from tension or overwhelming emotions. Speak with a mental health expert to research greater about this method and whether it is appropriate for you or a cherished one.

Sophie's DBT experience is truly one example of the way this treatment can assist young adults who war with emotional dysregulation. DBT is in particular effective for humans suffering from borderline character illness, however it may moreover assist human beings laid low with tension, depression, or located up-stressful pressure disorder.

DBT is characterized with the useful useful resource of blending elements of cognitive-behavioral treatment (CBT) with mindfulness practices. CBT is a form of remedy that specializes in changing terrible concept styles and behaviors, even as mindfulness practices assist human beings in final gift inside the 2d and managing their emotions. DBT offers an entire treatment plan by way of combining the ones techniques, which can assist people decorate their highbrow fitness and regular properly-being.

DBT is generally delivered in the form of institution remedy, despite the fact that individual treatment schooling may be included. Participants in employer remedy have a look at and exercise DBT capabilities with the assist of a knowledgeable therapist. This format is specifically beneficial for teens who can also experience remoted or disconnected from their friends.

If you or a cherished one is thinking about DBT, it's far important to find out a therapist who has acquired DBT training. Because DBT requires specialised education and certification, now not all therapists are certified to provide it. You can get a referral to a DBT expert out of your number one care medical medical physician or intellectual fitness issuer, or you could search for one on line.

Overall, DBT has the capability to be a life-changing treatment for youngsters suffering from tension and overwhelming feelings. Teens can enlarge the tools they need to control their intellectual fitness and assemble high-quality lives via studying mindfulness skills, knowledge emotion regulation, improving interpersonal talents, hard terrible mind, and the use of coping strategies. If you or a loved one is experiencing emotional dysregulation, communicate with a highbrow health expert right away to study more about how DBT can help.

COMMON MISCONCEPTIONS ABOUT DBT

DBT was firstly advanced to treat borderline character disorder (BPD), but it has given that been used to deal with a massive sort of intellectual fitness situations, together with despair, tension, ingesting issues, and substance abuse. Despite its awesome use and effectiveness, there are numerous myths about DBT that persist. In this section, we're able to debunk some of the maximum not unusual DBT myths and offer a greater correct records of this powerful remedy.

Myth #1: DBT Is Only for People with Borderline Personality Disorder

One of the maximum commonplace misconceptions about DBT is that it is fine suitable for humans suffering from borderline individual disorder (BPD). While DBT turn out to be to start with superior to cope with human beings with BPD, it has considering the reality that been adapted to address a big variety of highbrow fitness situations. DBT has been confirmed to be powerful inside the remedy of melancholy, tension, ingesting issues, substance abuse, and different intellectual ailments. Indeed, many folks who do not have BPD have found DBT beneficial in phrases of emotional law, interpersonal relationships, and fashionable first rate of existence.

Myth #2: DBT is Only for Women

Another extensively held misconception approximately DBT is that it's far best for ladies. This false impression is maximum probable due to the fact that BPD is identified greater frequently in girls than in guys. DBT, however, isn't always a gendered therapy and has been shown to be powerful in every males and females. DBT is primarily based on thoughts of mindfulness, emotional regulation, distress tolerance, and interpersonal effectiveness that follow to all of us, regardless of gender.

Myth #3: DBT is a Quick Fix

DBT is not a panacea. It is a protracted-time period, huge therapy that requires a enormous effort and time determination. Individual therapy commands, enterprise treatment intervals, and homework assignments are commonplace additives of DBT. Individual remedy lessons are designed to help patients enhance their emotional law, misery tolerance, and interpersonal effectiveness. Individuals can exercising those competencies and gather comments from their buddies in a supportive environment ultimately of group remedy training. Homework assignments are intended to reinforce treatment talents and assist humans in making use of them in their each day lives.

While DBT can be especially powerful in improving mental fitness consequences, it is not a quick repair and necessitates a big time and effort funding.

Myth #4: DBT is Solely Concerned with Mindfulness

Mindfulness is an important problem of DBT, but it isn't always the handiest one. DBT is a multifaceted treatment that mixes an entire lot of talents and techniques to assist people enhance their emotional regulation, misery tolerance, and interpersonal effectiveness. DBT consists of, further to mindfulness, skills for emotion regulation, interpersonal effectiveness, and misery tolerance. Individuals with emotional law talents can choose out and manage their feelings in a wholesome way. Individuals with interpersonal effectiveness capabilities are better capable to speak with others and shape wholesome relationships. Individuals with misery tolerance capabilities can tolerate and address distressing conditions in a healthful manner.

Myth #5: DBT is Only for Teenagers

DBT is not only for teenagers. While DBT became to begin with designed for teens with borderline man or woman ailment, it has for the cause that been tailored for use with human beings of every age. DBT has been hooked up to be powerful in treating intellectual health troubles in every old and young people. In reality, a few research indicates that DBT may be particularly effective in treating depression and anxiety in older adults.

Myth #6: DBT is Only for People Suffering from Severe Mental Illnesses

DBT isn't first-rate for people with excessive highbrow ailments. While DBT is frequently used to deal with people with immoderate mental illnesses, it can also assist human beings with a whole lot a lot less intense mental ailments. DBT can help human beings enhance their emotional law, pressure control, and interpersonal relationships. It additionally can be used as a preventative measure to help individuals in developing resilience and coping competencies in advance than pressure turns into overwhelming.

Myth #7: DBT is Only Effective for People Who Attend Therapy Regularly

While regular attendance at treatment intervals is crucial for DBT sufferers, it isn't the first-rate detail that determines its effectiveness. DBT is supposed to teach humans the abilities and techniques they want to manipulate their intellectual fitness on their very very own. While attending treatment lessons can assist to enhance those capabilities and acquire remarks from a educated therapist, humans can also observe these abilties outside of treatment durations and observe huge improvements in their highbrow fitness.

Chapter 8: Finding A Qualified Dbt Therapist Or Program

Dialectical conduct therapy (DBT) has been tested to be powerful in the treatment of hundreds of highbrow fitness situations, which includes borderline character disorder, despair, tension, substance abuse, and ingesting problems. DBT is a complete and evidence-based totally absolutely actually therapy that mixes elements of cognitive-behavioral remedy, mindfulness, and dialectics to help human beings alter their emotions, decorate their interpersonal relationships, and stay a better lifestyles.

Finding a certified DBT therapist or software, then again, may be a tough task, specially for oldsters which might be new to remedy or have confined get proper of entry to to intellectual fitness offerings. Thus, in this segment, we're capable of flow over a number of the most critical elements to don't forget whilst seeking out a DBT therapist or software.

Before we get into the specifics of locating an authorized DBT therapist or software, it's far crucial to speedy apprehend what DBT is and the way it really works. DBT have become advanced in the Eighties thru psychologist Marsha Linehan to help humans with borderline individual sickness, but it has considering that been tailored to address a wonderful form of intellectual fitness situations.

DBT is a capabilities-based totally absolutely treatment that specializes in four center talents: mindfulness, distress tolerance, emotion law, and interpersonal effectiveness. These competencies are taught in everyone remedy intervals and abilties corporations, and that they may be implemented to a large kind of regular conditions.

DBT is a collaborative therapy in which the therapist and the affected man or woman collaborate to discover intricate behaviors and concept patterns and growth techniques for handling them. The therapist acts as a train and manual, assisting the affected character in developing competencies and a more enjoy of self-interest and self-compassion.

Finding a Qualified DBT Therapist

There are severa important factors to keep in mind at the identical time as searching out a certified DBT therapist. First and essential, search for a DBT-knowledgeable and certified therapist. Because DBT is a specialized treatment that necessitates unique education and data, it's miles crucial to find a therapist who has formal training within the method. The DBT-Linehan Board of Certification is in price of certifying DBT therapists, so you can take a look at their internet site to peer if a therapist is certified.

Second, it's miles critical to discover a therapist who has worked with the precise highbrow fitness scenario for that you are searching for treatment. While DBT may be used to address severa situations, it's miles essential to find out a therapist who has labored with people who have comparable goals and traumatic situations.

Third, it's far important to discover a therapist with whom you experience snug. Because remedy is a collaborative technique that necessitates accept as authentic with and open verbal exchange, it's far vital to discover a therapist with whom you experience you may develop a sturdy jogging relationship. Many therapists offer loose consultations or initial durations, that can assist you decide whether or now not you are snug with them.

Fourth, sensible factors which includes location, availability, and price must be considered. Finding a therapist who is resultseasily located and has availability that suits collectively along with your time table can be vital for preserving consistency in your remedy. It is also essential to recollect the rate of remedy, as DBT may be greater considerable and lengthy-time period than different methods.

Finding a DBT Program

DBT may be introduced in the shape of a program this is composed of every person remedy and competencies agencies in addition to character remedy. There are numerous important factors to preserve in mind whilst searching out a DBT application.

First and primary, look for an entire application that consists of each individual treatment and competencies companies. Because DBT is a talents-based definitely treatment, it's miles critical to discover a software program that consists of every additives.

Second, look for a software program program this is led thru the usage of licensed and expert DBT therapists. As with character therapy, it's miles important to find a software program led by way of therapists who have acquired DBT training and certification further to experience strolling with the suitable intellectual fitness situations for which you are seeking out treatment.

Third, it is important to keep in mind this device's shape and format. Some DBT applications are extensive, with multiple treatment and capabilities enterprise business enterprise training consistent with week, even as others are greater traditional, with weekly treatment and skills organisation instructions. It is essential to undergo in thoughts which format will exquisite meet your requirements and paintings collectively with your agenda.

Fourth, endure in thoughts this device's price, as DBT applications may be greater pricey than person remedy. Some applications may be included with the beneficial resource of insurance, even as others can also necessitate out-of-pocket expenses.

How to Get the Most Out of DBT Therapy

There are several hints that permit you to get the most from your treatment, whether or not or not you are seeking out man or woman remedy or a DBT utility.

To begin, it's miles vital to technique therapy with an open mind and a choice to examine and develop. DBT is a competencies-based totally definitely treatment, due to this that that the talents you studies inside the treatment may be achieved to a huge sort of conditions for your each day existence. However, growing those skills takes effort and time, so it's far essential to technique remedy with a willingness to place inside the attempt.

Second, it's miles essential to be open and sincere collectively with your therapist. Therapy is a stable and unique environment wherein you could discover your mind and feelings, and it is vital that you are honest and open collectively with your therapist in case you want to get the maximum out of your treatment.

Third, it is vital to vicinity the skills you examine in the remedy into workout out of doors of the remedy instructions. DBT capabilities are imagined to be utilized in ordinary situations, and schooling them outdoor of the remedy will let you gain mastery and self belief within the use of them.

Fourth, it is essential to engage in self-care and self-compassion. DBT emphasizes self-care and self-compassion, and it's far crucial to prioritize self-care so as to hold your highbrow fitness and nicely-being.

Chapter 9: Setting Goals And Tracking Progress In Dbt

DBT is a whole remedy method that consists of purpose setting and development monitoring to ensure that people are making good sized improvement in the direction of their favored results. In this sub-phase, we can speak the significance of intention putting and monitoring improvement in DBT, as well as sensible suggestions for incorporating those techniques into your remedy plan.

Perez turn out to be generally a chunk of a troublemaker. He turned into in no way one to observe recommendations or persist with timetables. But as he approached young adults, he found out that his lack of shape have become stifling him. He desired to make changes in his life, however he changed into uncertain in which to start. That is whilst he observed DBT, or dialectical behavior remedy.

Perez emerge as to begin with skeptical. He didn't similar to the idea of remedy, and he specifically did now not just like the concept of putting goals and retaining tune of his development. However, after a few durations, he commenced to look the benefit. He decided out that by means of way of way of placing desires and maintaining song of his development, he need to really alternate his lifestyles.

The first step emerge as to set goals. Perez had in no way given an awful lot idea to what he desired to carry out in life. Sure, he had some indistinct notions, collectively with trying to acquire success and glad, but he had in no way definitely sat down and brought into consideration what those ideas meant to him.

Perez started out out to set a few particular, measurable, manageable, relevant, and time-certain (SMART) goals with the assist of his therapist. He resolved to raise his grades, spend less time on his cellular phone, and take a look at a brand new potential. These dreams had been all unique and measurable, permitting him to music his development and observe how a ways he had come.

The following step turned into to track his improvement. Perez initially positioned this element hard. He despised the idea of having to hold track of everything he did. However, his therapist described that tracking his development changed into vital to carrying out his dreams. He need to see wherein he emerge as succeeding and in which he needed to improve by means of manner of retaining a document of his movements.

Perez chose to start with the goal of improving his grades. He set a cause for himself to get a B or higher in all of his education thru using the cease of the semester. To keep tune of his development, he made a chart that indexed all of his instructions and the grades he received on each task. In addition, he covered his traditional grade for each class.

Perez to start with found it difficult to hold music of the whole thing. He fast realized, however, that through devoting a few minutes every day to updating his chart, he need to without troubles see how he modified into progressing. He determined that once he can also need to look his progress, he end up more encouraged to look at and complete assignments.

Tracking his progress furthermore helped Perez understand areas wherein he had to improve. For instance, he determined that he turned into having issue in his math magnificence. He have to see from his chart that he have been struggling along together with his math assignments. This induced him to are seeking out extra help from his teacher and commit extra time to reading for his math assessments.

Perez became an increasing number of inspired to set and attain dreams as he commenced to appearance the cease give up result of his hard paintings. He commenced to spend a whole lot much less time on his cellphone and in addition time working in the direction of his new competencies, guitar gambling. He decided that he became having greater fun in existence and that he had a experience of cause that he had in no way had earlier than.

However, Perez's journey became not without problems. He felt like giving up at instances whilst he wasn't getting the results he favored or while he emerge as crushed through the quantity of exertions he needed to do. However, he recognized that setbacks had been a natural part of the manner and that he should look at from them.

Perez's assist machine became one of the factors that helped him stay heading within the right path. Of direction, he had his therapist, but he additionally had his buddies and family. They cheered him on whilst he modified into down and celebrated his victories with him.

Perez in the long run carried out his aim of receiving a B or higher in all of his education. He furthermore learned a way to set and song dreams and development, and he discovered that doing so allowed him to make first-rate modifications in his life. He changed into pleased with himself and his achievements, and he knew he had the equipment to set and gain desires within the future.

Perez's DBT revel in taught him that motive-placing and development monitoring were no longer simplest for adults. They were useful tools for young adults to use if you want to make top notch changes of their lives. He decided to percent his enjoy with other teens and inspire them to try DBT for themselves.

Perez started out out out thru manner of telling his friends and circle of relatives about his ordeal. He mentioned his dreams and development with them, similarly to how DBT had helped him collect them. He additionally advocated them to set goals and music their development, and he supplied to assist them in getting started.

Then Perez decided to transport one step in addition. He installation a social media account to share his story and connect to different teens inquisitive about DBT. He began out thru sharing photos of his improvement charts and updates on his goals. He also provided recommendation and tips for placing and reaching desires, and he advocated his fans to percent their very personal testimonies.

Perez's social media account quick grew in reputation, masses to his marvel. His story stimulated teenagers everywhere within the worldwide, and they have been keen to attempt DBT for themselves. They informed Perez about their non-public dreams and progress, and he supplied encouragement and help.

Perez speedy had a community of young adults who had been all operating in the path of their goals and keeping song in their development. They shared their successes and disasters, and that they presented advice and beneficial aid at the identical time as essential. Perez turned into proud to have created this form of immoderate fine and scary environment for teens, and he knew he had made a difference in their lives.

Perez's experience examined that teens, like adults, have to set and gain desires. They should make high-quality modifications of their lives and enjoy more on top of things of their future with the useful resource of the use of DBT strategies collectively with reason-putting and improvement tracking. Teenagers like Perez ought to overcome barriers and benefit their goals with the assist of a therapist, buddies, and family.

Perez in the long run determined out that setting and carrying out desires became about more than surely getting somewhere. It grow to be all about the adventure and the development that got here with it. Perez positioned that he grow to be able to an lousy lot extra than he had previously imagined via the use of manner of pushing himself to set and accumulate dreams. He felt greater confident, inspired, and in control of his existence. And he changed into nicely aware that the sky changed into the limit for what he need to accomplish inside the destiny.

Why Set Goals in DBT?

Setting dreams is an essential part of DBT as it enables people set up a smooth path for his or her treatment and create a plan for his or her recovery journey. Individuals can discover what they preference to attain of their remedy with the aid of the use of setting goals, which enables them stay prompted and targeted on their preferred consequences. Furthermore, purpose-putting offers the treatment machine a revel in of cause and because of this, which can be extraordinarily empowering and assist humans experience greater on pinnacle of things of their lives.

It is crucial to set precise, measurable, workable, relevant, and time-high quality (SMART) goals whilst present process DBT. These desires ought to be tailored to the character's precise desires and dreams, in addition to being regular with their values and priorities. Some examples of SMART dreams in DBT may additionally moreover encompass the subsequent:

Within the subsequent six months, lessen the frequency of self-damage behaviors with the aid of half of of.

Participate in all DBT institution intervals over the following 3 months.

Attend a verbal exchange competencies workshop within the subsequent month to enhance your communique abilties.

Practice self-care sports sports for as a minimum 30 minutes every day to increase self-compassion.

Improve your emotional regulation abilties through using doing 10 mins of mindfulness physical sports each day.

Chapter 10: Tracking Progress In Dbt

It is vital to song improvement in the course of undertaking goals after they were installation. Individuals and their therapists can track development to determine whether or not or now not or no longer their treatment plan is powerful and to become aware of areas that would require additional assist or changes. It additionally assists people in very last chargeable for their improvement and celebrating their accomplishments along the way.

In DBT, there are numerous processes to track improvement, which encompass:

1. Diary Cards

Diary playing cards are a famous DBT device which could assist humans keep tune in their emotions, behaviors, and remedy dreams on a every day basis. Diary playing gambling playing cards usually encompass a listing of feelings, which includes anger, unhappiness, or tension, similarly to a score scale for each emotion's depth. Individuals also can use diary gambling playing cards to preserve music in their personal behaviors, which includes self-harm, substance abuse, or impulsive spending. Diary cards can help select out patterns and triggers for poor behaviors through offering a image of an man or woman's improvement over the years.

2. Progress Journals

In DBT, improvement journals can be a useful tool for monitoring development in the route of specific desires. Individuals can use improvement journals to track their improvement in the path of desires, reflect on their successes and demanding situations, and find out regions for development. Individuals can use improvement journals to stay stimulated and targeted on their dreams, similarly to to keep song in their progress over the years.

3. Outcome Measures

Outcome measures are standardized exams used to track someone's development towards unique treatment goals. To music development over time, very last consequences measures may be administered at normal periods, inclusive of every month or every six months. The Beck Depression Inventory, the Difficulties in Emotion Regulation Scale, and the Borderline Evaluation of Severity Over Time (BEST) Scale are three generally used very last effects measures in DBT.

Tips for Setting Goals and Tracking Progress in DBT

1. Work together along side your Therapist

In DBT, setting goals and tracking improvement is a collaborative tool many of the affected individual and their therapist. It is essential to collaborate together with your therapist to extend dreams which might be significant and relevant for your unique desires and dreams. Furthermore, your therapist can provide guidance and resource as you parent in the direction of your goals, in addition to help you in identifying areas for improvement and adjusting your remedy plan for this reason.

2. Start Small

When placing desires in DBT, it can be useful first of all small, conceivable dreams in advance than progressing to extra hard ones. Starting small can help you gain momentum and offer a revel in of achievement, each of which may be extremely motivating. Also, attaining smaller desires can help humans advantage self guarantee and enlarge the capabilities needed to tackle huge dreams within the destiny.

three. Celebrate Successes

Tracking development in DBT is ready celebrating successes further to figuring out areas for development. It is important to recognize and feature a laugh improvement inside the route of desires, irrespective of how small. Celebrating successes can assist human beings stay inspired and offer a feel of feat, which could help them live heading inside the proper route to achieve their desires.

4. Stay Flexible

Individuals ought to live flexible as they improvement through their remedy plan, adjusting desires and treatment strategies as wished. DBT is a dynamic manner, and dreams and remedy strategies may also want to be adjusted as an character's development and wishes alternate. Staying bendy and open to modifications can assist people stay at the proper tune in the direction of their desires and acquire prolonged-time period exchange.

Goal putting and progress tracking are essential components of DBT that could assist humans in making meaningful development within the route in their desired consequences. Individuals can live stimulated and focused on their restoration adventure through the usage of way of setting precise, measurable, possible, applicable, and time-positive goals and monitoring improvement with device together with diary playing cards.

Chapter 11: Basic Terms On Dbt

What Is DBT?

DBT stands for Dialectical Behavior Therapy. It is a shape of treatment that helps human beings expands new capabilities and strategies to manipulate their feelings, relationships, and life traumatic situations more efficiently.

In smooth phrases, DBT helps human beings discover ways to apprehend and adjust their feelings, cope with stress, and beautify their relationships with others. It includes a mixture of man or woman treatment lessons and organization talents schooling wherein humans study specific strategies to deal with hard situations.

The "dialectical" a part of DBT method finding a balance between popularity and trade. It encourages accepting your self as you are on the identical time as also running closer to splendid adjustments in your thoughts, behaviors, and emotions.

DBT is often used to help folks that warfare with severe emotions, self-negative behaviors, borderline character sickness, and one in every of a type intellectual health situations. It offers

realistic equipment and strategies to navigate lifestyles's traumatic situations and construct a lifestyles worth residing.

Components/Modules Of DBT:

There are essentially four modules/additives of DBT.

Mindfulness

Distress Tolerance

Emotion Regulation

Interpersonal effectiveness

Below are clean elements of each of the modules:

1. Mindfulness:

Mindfulness is ready being surely aware and present inside the modern-day-day 2nd without judgement. In DBT, mindfulness capabilities are taught to assist human beings take note of their thoughts, feelings, and sensations with out getting crushed. It consists of schooling techniques like deep breathing, meditation, and searching at one's studies with out reacting .

2. Distress Tolerance:

Distress tolerance abilties consciousness on assisting humans deal with distressing situations after they can not exchange or keep away from them. These skills teach people a way to tolerate emotional ache, strain, and hard instances with out making impulsive or dangerous selections. Examples of distress tolerance abilities include self-soothing sports activities, distraction strategies, and mastering to journey out extreme emotions.

3. Emotion Regulation:

Emotion regulation capabilities assist people recognize, manipulate, and trade severe or overwhelming emotions. People discover ways to discover and label their emotions, recognize triggers, and increase more wholesome techniques of managing emotional u.S.And downs. These abilties contain techniques which encompass trouble-solving, expressing emotions correctly, and appealing in sports activities that promote emotional properly-being.

4. Interpersonal Effectiveness:

Interpersonal effectiveness talents interest on improving relationships and verbal exchange with others. This module facilitates humans enlarge assertiveness, set healthful obstacles, and navigate conflicts in a exceptional manner. It teaches effective communication strategies, negotiation capabilities, and techniques to construct and keep healthy relationships.

These four modules are an critical part of DBT and provide humans with a entire set of tools to govern their emotions, cope with distress, and enhance their relationships with themselves and others.

DBT Module Rationale And How It Contributes To Treatment:

Dialectical Behavior Therapy (DBT) is a shape of remedy that became on the begin superior to cope with humans with borderline persona sickness (BPD). It has thinking about that been tailor-made for various unique intellectual health situations. DBT consists of several modules, each with its very own particular purpose and contribution to ordinary treatment effectiveness. Here's a simplified clarification of the reason behind every module and the manner it lets in in remedy:

1. Mindfulness:

Mindfulness is the muse of DBT. It includes taking note of the triumphing 2d without judgment. This module goals to help people enlarge attention of their thoughts, feelings, and bodily sensations. By being extra conscious, people can learn how to observe and accumulate their opinions, which can lessen emotional reactivity and enhance their capability to reply efficiently to tough situations.

2. Distress Tolerance:

Distress tolerance abilties consciousness on helping human beings address and tolerate distressing conditions without resorting to risky or impulsive behaviors. The module teaches abilties collectively with self-soothing, distraction strategies, and recognition of reality. By studying to tolerate misery with out accomplishing unfavorable behaviors, individuals can save you crises and make more healthful alternatives.

three. Emotion Regulation:

This module permits people apprehend and manage their emotions efficiently. It teaches abilties for identifying and labeling emotions, information the abilities of emotions, and converting emotional responses. By acquiring emotion law capabilities, human beings can reduce emotional intensity, growth remarkable feelings, and keep away from emotional vulnerability.

four. Interpersonal Effectiveness:

Interpersonal effectiveness competencies assist human beings increase healthful relationships and navigate social interactions. This module specializes in assertiveness, effective verbal exchange, setting obstacles, and resolving conflicts. By enhancing their interpersonal talents, people can set up and maintain nice relationships, that could decorate their normal nicely-being.

In addition to those modules, character treatment durations and a consultation institution for the therapist also are vital elements of DBT. Individual remedy offers a supportive and collaborative area for addressing unique problems and strolling toward remedy dreams. The session employer offers help and guidance to the therapist, ensuring they live stimulated and powerful in their transport of DBT.

Overall, the reason within the lower lower back of every module of DBT is to offer human beings with a whole set of abilties and strategies to efficaciously manage their emotions, tolerate distress, enhance relationships, and stay a extra pleasurable life. By combining mindfulness, misery tolerance, emotion law, and interpersonal effectiveness, DBT pursuits to empower people to navigate life's worrying situations with more resilience and well-being.

Emotional Regulation Skills In DBT

Dialectical Behavioural Therapy has five critical emotional law talents;

Understanding Emotions in DBT

Identifying and Labeling Emotions

Opposite Action: Changing Emotional Responses

Building Positive Emotional Experiences

Navigating Complex Emotional Patterns

Understanding Emotions In DBT:

Here's a be conscious on knowledge feelings and their competencies in terms of Dialectical Behavior Therapy (DBT):

Emotions play a big feature in our lives, influencing our thoughts, movements, and regular well-being. In Dialectical Behavior Therapy (DBT), emotions are considered as critical symptoms that provide valuable statistics approximately our internal reviews and the area around us. Understanding emotions and their abilities is a important issue of DBT, aimed closer to promoting emotional regulation and improving trendy mental fitness.

1. Validating Emotions: DBT emphasizes the importance of validating our emotions, acknowledging that all feelings are legitimate and serve a motive. Even if an emotion appears overwhelming or uncomfortable, it's miles vital to just accept and validate it as a

proper response to our memories. Validating emotions allows us amplify a non-judgmental attitude closer to ourselves, fostering self-compassion and self-beauty.

2. Identifying Primary and Secondary Emotions: DBT acknowledges that emotions can frequently be complex and layered. Primary emotions are the preliminary, instantaneous reactions we enjoy, which incorporates anger, worry, unhappiness, or joy. Secondary feelings, as an alternative, are next emotions that upward thrust up in reaction to primary feelings, frequently pushed via judgments, expectancies, or beliefs. By figuring out each number one and secondary feelings, we're able to benefit a deeper knowledge of our emotional critiques and cope with underlying problems efficaciously.

3. Emotional Functionality: Every emotion serves a reason, however the reality that it is able to not always be obvious. DBT focuses on know-how the useful components of feelings.

For instance, anger can encourage us to set obstacles, disappointment can mean a need for consolation and useful resource, and fear can signal functionality danger. By spotting the feature of feelings, we are capable of respond to them in greater wholesome and further adaptive techniques, using them as guideposts for problem-fixing and self-care.

four. Emotion Regulation: DBT gives practical techniques to enhance emotional regulation talents. By growing effective coping mechanisms, people can manipulate and reply to feelings in a way that aligns with their prolonged-time period goals. Techniques like mindfulness, misery tolerance, and interpersonal effectiveness help human beings assemble resilience and reduce emotional vulnerability, main to extra healthy emotional responses and superior regular properly-being.

five. Building a Life Worth Living: Ultimately, DBT interests to assist humans construct a existence nicely well worth living, even in the face of hard emotions and situations. Understanding feelings and their skills empowers individuals to make knowledgeable picks, domesticate sizeable relationships, and pursue private values and goals. By integrating emotional recognition and law into each day life, DBT fosters emotional nicely-being, resilience, and private growth.

Remember, knowledge feelings and their abilities is a journey that takes time and practice. With the help of DBT, humans can expand a greater experience of emotional self-popularity, navigate difficult emotions greater successfully, and cultivate a more pleasurable life.

Identifying and Labeling Emotions:

In Dialectical Behavior Therapy (DBT), identifying and labeling feelings is a essential step inside the course of expertise and managing them effectively. DBT emphasizes the significance of recognizing and validating our feelings as a way to growth emotional intelligence and address misery. Here's a easy examine on identifying and labeling emotions in phrases of DBT:

Identifying emotions: In DBT, identifying feelings consists of turning into aware about what we are feeling at any given 2nd. It's about listening to the physical sensations, mind, and behaviors related to our feelings. This requires being present inside the 2d and tuning in to our inner studies. We can become aware of emotions through asking ourselves questions like "What am I feeling proper now?" or "What is the primary emotion I'm experiencing?"

Labeling emotions: Once we've got diagnosed an emotion, the following step is to label it. This manner giving a name or a label to the emotion we're experiencing. In DBT, there may be a particular set of center feelings which are typically used for labeling, together with anger, unhappiness, fear, happiness, disgust, and wonder. However, it is vital to be aware that emotions may be complex and nuanced, so we would use more precise labels like frustration, tension, or pleasure to offer an explanation for our emotional nation as it must be.

Why is it important: Identifying and labeling emotions in DBT is critical for numerous motives. Firstly, it permits us turn out to be extra self-aware and advantage a deeper know-how of ourselves. By efficaciously figuring out and labeling our feelings, we are able to higher talk our goals and evaluations to others. Secondly, it permits us to validate and receive our emotions with out judgment, it surely is a essential trouble of emotional law. Lastly, labeling emotions permits us apprehend styles and triggers, permitting us to enlarge powerful coping techniques to manage distress and decorate our emotional properly-being.

Overall, identifying and labeling emotions in DBT is a vital capability that allows emotional reputation and law. It empowers humans to widely recognized and apprehend their emotions, foremost to greater healthy coping mechanisms and improved interpersonal relationships.

Opposite Action: Changing Emotional Responses

Opposite Action is a key concept in Dialectical Behavior Therapy (DBT) that enables individuals change their emotional responses. It entails intentionally appearing in a way this is contrary to how they will actually react to their feelings. This technique is particularly useful for coping with severe or unwanted feelings and reducing their bad impact on one's nicely-being. The idea behind Opposite Action is that our emotions frequently force us closer to great behaviors that won't be useful or useful in the long run. For instance, if someone is feeling sad and withdrawn, they will be inclined to isolate themselves in addition. However, thru using Opposite Action, they'll deliberately select to interact in sports that deliver them pride or be a part of them with others, together with going out with friends or taking element in a interest.

By deliberately performing opposite to the preliminary emotional urge, people can disrupt the cycle of horrible feelings and create space for more excessive nice opinions. Opposite Action allows people construct emotional resilience and increase extra healthful coping mechanisms through hard the automatic response driven through their feelings.

It is essential to note that Opposite Action does no longer reason to deny or suppress emotions. Instead, it encourages human beings to reply in a manner that promotes emotional well-being and lets in them flow into in the route in their goals. Through consistent exercising, Opposite Action can result in a shift in emotional patterns, allowing humans to revel in greater emotional stability and make more optimistic choices of their lives.

Building Positive Emotional Experiences:

In DBT, building excessive first rate emotional reports is an important thing of cultivating emotional well-being and resilience. The goal is to decorate our ability to experience awesome emotions, that might make a contribution to a extra balanced and first-class life.

To construct effective emotional testimonies, we are able to start with the aid of project sports activities activities that convey us delight, delight, or a revel in of achievement. It's approximately consciously choosing to do matters that uplift our spirits and create high-quality emotions. This would likely contain pursuing pastimes or pursuits we adore, spending time with cherished ones, conducting physical exercise, or education relaxation strategies.

Furthermore, mindfulness performs a critical characteristic in DBT. It encourages us to be without a doubt gift inside the 2nd, taking note of our mind, emotions, and sensations without judgment. By operating in the direction of mindfulness, we're capable of become more aware about the powerful elements of our lives that we often neglect and get delight from them deeply. It allows us to apprehend the smooth joys and splendor around us, along side the warm temperature of daylight, the flavor of a scrumptious meal, or the sound of laughter.

Another vital thing of building notable emotional memories is growing a top notch attitude. It entails difficult terrible thoughts and actively cultivating effective thoughts and beliefs. By reframing terrible situations, that specialize in our strengths, and education gratitude, we can shift our angle in the direction of a greater best outlook on life. In addition, nurturing healthful relationships is critical. Surrounding ourselves with supportive and effective folks who uplift us can substantially effect our emotional nicely-being. Building and maintaining strong social connections, expressing care and appreciation for others, and searching out help while needed make contributions to superb emotional studies.

Lastly, self-care is essential for constructing great emotional studies. Taking care of our physical, emotional, and highbrow properly-being is vital. Engaging in sports that sell self-care, together with getting enough sleep, consuming nutritious meals, working toward relaxation strategies, and appealing in sports activities that bring us pleasure, can help us gather great emotional stories.

Remember, constructing high-quality emotional reviews is a manner that calls for workout and self-compassion. By incorporating the ones techniques into our lives, we are capable of regularly cultivate a extra high-quality and enjoyable emotional usa.

Managing Complex Emotions:

Emotions can be a complicated and sometimes overwhelming part of our lives. They are available unique sizes and patterns, starting from joy and delight to unhappiness and anger. However, a few humans revel in severe feelings that can be tough to recognize and control. This is in which DBT may be pretty useful.

DBT is a recuperation approach that makes a speciality of coaching human beings skills to navigate and modify their feelings effectively. When it includes complex emotional patterns, there are a few key elements to keep in thoughts.

Firstly, it is vital to recognize and end up aware about the feelings you're experiencing. This can also sound smooth, but every now and then feelings may be complex and muddled. DBT emphasizes the importance of knowledge your feelings and being capable of label them accurately. By doing so, you could advantage clarity and a higher understanding of what you are going through.

Secondly, DBT emphasizes the idea of reputation. It recognizes that every one feelings are legitimate and that it is natural to revel in more than a few emotions. Rather than trying to suppress or ignore emotions, DBT encourages humans to accept them with out judgment. Acceptance would not endorse you have to like or don't forget the emotion, but it permits you to widely recognized its presence and flow into in advance.

Thirdly, DBT teaches abilties to regulate and manage extreme feelings correctly. These talents can encompass mindfulness, distress tolerance, emotion regulation, and interpersonal effectiveness. Mindfulness allows people live gift inside the moment and study their feelings with out getting overwhelmed. Distress tolerance equips human beings with strategies to tolerate distressing situations without resorting to unstable behaviors. Emotion regulation skills awareness on information and modulating emotions, on the same time as interpersonal effectiveness talents teach powerful communication and courting-building strategies.

Lastly, navigating complicated emotional styles also entails growing a assist device. DBT emphasizes the significance of seeking out assist from relied on individuals, together with buddies, circle of relatives, or a therapist. Having a supportive community can offer comfort, steerage, and encouragement all through difficult instances.

Remember, navigating complicated emotional styles takes time and exercising. DBT offers valuable tools and techniques to help you in this journey. By studying to recognize, get hold of, regulate, and are looking for help, you can amplify a more sense of emotional properly-being and resilience.

Dialectics In DBT

What Is Dialectics?

Dialectics in DBT can be defined as the popularity and attractiveness of opposing or contradictory truths, mind, or views, with the reason of locating a synthesis or resolution that balances popularity and change. It involves shielding multiple views concurrently and navigating dialectical dilemmas to promote private growth and emotional nicely-being. In DBT, dialectics are used to help humans increase a more balanced and bendy way of wondering, feeling, and behaving. It includes finding a center floor amongst apparently contradictory positions, in vicinity of seeing subjects in black and white or both-or terms. Dialectics encourage people to preserve more than one perspectives simultaneously and find a synthesis or decision that consists of every viewpoints.

Benefits Of Dialectics And How It Affects Treatment:

Dialectics in DBT are important because of the reality they assist individuals in treatment, increase a extra balanced and bendy way of questioning, feeling, and behaving. Here's how dialectics have an impact on remedy:

Chapter 12: More On Dbt Modules

An Overview of Skills Taught and Their Applications on Each DBT Module:

DBT (Dialectical Behavior Therapy) is a therapeutic approach that combines cognitive-behavioral strategies with mindfulness practices. It is generally designed to help folks who warfare with extreme feelings, impulsive behaviors, and issues in keeping strong relationships. DBT includes numerous modules, every focused on specific areas of capability improvement. Here's a top degree view of each module and the skills taught inner them:

1. Mindfulness:

Mindfulness is the foundation of DBT and lets in humans boom recognition and splendor of the existing 2d. It teaches talents for looking at, describing and taking component in critiques with out judgement. Mindfulness abilities beautify self-attention, emotional regulation, and the capability to tolerate distress.

2. Interpersonal Effectiveness:

This module focuses on improving conversation and courting talents. It teaches humans the way to assertively unique their dreams, set boundaries, and navigate conflicts. Interpersonal effectiveness competencies also embody techniques for constructing and keeping healthy relationships, which encompass energetic listening and problem-solving.

three. Emotion Regulation:

Emotion regulation capabilities intention to assist human beings grow to be aware about, understand, and manipulate their emotions efficaciously. Techniques taught on this module include emotion focus, figuring out triggers and vulnerabilities, tough unhelpful thoughts, and the use of healthful coping techniques. Emotion law abilities empower humans to tolerate distressing feelings and prevent impulsive behaviors.

four. Distress Tolerance:

Distress tolerance skills are crucial for managing excessive emotions with out resorting to unstable or impulsive movements. These abilties cognizance on growing misery tolerance thru getting to know to tolerate emotional pain, training self-soothing strategies, and accepting conditions that cannot be modified. Distress tolerance capabilities moreover include crisis survival techniques and building a repertoire of healthful coping mechanisms.

There is one extra module practiced in some remedy periods, this is "core mindfulness".

5. Core Mindfulness:

Core mindfulness builds upon the foundation installation within the initial mindfulness module. It emphasizes cultivating a non-judgmental mind-set, developing an searching at self, and deepening mindfulness exercise. Core mindfulness capabilities are designed to boom self-reputation, lessen emotional reactivity, and promote a enjoy of calm and popularity.

Each module of DBT is interconnected and builds upon the others to provide a entire set of competencies for people. The overarching motive is to help people enlarge a balanced and effective method to coping with feelings, relationships, and life disturbing conditions. DBT is generally used within the remedy of borderline persona sickness, however its strategies can also benefit individuals with various different mental fitness conditions and problems with emotional regulation.

Practical Examples And Exercises For Each DBT Module:

1. Mindfulness:

Mindful Breathing:

Sit quietly and interest your interest for your breath. Notice the sensation of every inhale and exhale, without in search of to change it. If your mind wanders, gently convey your attention again for your breath.

Body Scan:

Close your eyes and bring your hobby to particular additives of your body, beginning out of your toes and moving upward. Notice any sensations or anxiety you is probably feeling without judgment.

2. Interpersonal Effectiveness:

DEAR MAN:

Practice assertiveness through the use of the DEAR MAN acronym. Describe the state of affairs, particular your feelings, assert your desires, deliver a boost on your aspect of view, stay Mindful of your aim, Appear confident, and Negotiate for a compromise.

Active Listening:

Engage in a conversation with a pal or member of the family and workout active listening. Give your whole attention, hold eye touch, and summarize or reflect on what the character is saying to reveal understanding.

3. Emotion Regulation:

Emotion Labeling:

Throughout the day, test in with yourself and label the feelings you are experiencing. Write them down and reflect on what delivered about those emotions.

Opposite Action:

Identify an emotion you need to alternate (e.G., anger) and consider the corresponding opposite emotion (e.G., calmness). Engage in sports activities that evoke the alternative emotion, consisting of taking a calming bathtub or paying attention to calming song.

4. Distress Tolerance:

Self-Soothing:

Create a self-soothing package deal packed with items that provide comfort, which incorporates scented candles, moderate blankets, or a favourite e-book. Use those devices while you are feeling harassed or overwhelmed.

Urge Surfing:

When confronted with a sturdy urge or yearning, accept as true with your self as a surfer the usage of a wave. Observe the urge without performing on it, allowing it to upward push and fall manifestly, just like a wave.

five. Core Mindfulness:

Non-Judgmental Observation:

Choose an object, at the facet of a flower or a chunk of fruit. Spend a couple of minutes searching at it intently, being attentive to its shades, textures, and shapes. Practice watching without judgement or assessment.

Three-Minute Breathing Space:

Take three minutes to pause and convey your attention on your breath. Notice the sensations of your breath coming in and going out. Observe any thoughts or sensations that rise up without getting caught up in them.

These sporting sports provide a glimpse into the realistic utility of DBT capabilities.

Remember, consistency and practice are key to developing skillability in those skills.

Chapter 13: Application Of Dbt

DBT in Therapy Settings:

DBT or Dialectical Behavior Therapy is usually done in diverse settings which incorporate;

Individual remedy

Group therapy

Skills training

Below is a easy rationalization of the way DBT is used in each putting:

1. Individual Therapy:

In person treatment, a person works one-on-one with a knowledgeable therapist. The therapist allows the person grow to be privy to and understand their emotional struggles, together with excessive mood swings or problem regulating emotions. They train unique capabilities and techniques to cope with the ones feelings successfully. This can encompass techniques like mindfulness, emotional regulation, distress tolerance, and interpersonal effectiveness. Individual remedy allows for customized attention and tailored treatment plans to cope with the person's particular goals and desires.

2. Group Therapy:

Group remedy involves a small organization of people who come collectively with one or extra therapists to talk about and work on their emotional stressful conditions. In a DBT organization treatment setting, people percentage their tales, study from every different, and workout utilizing the DBT skills they have found out. The group environment gives a supportive network in which human beings can discover ways to validate and empathize with others, growth interpersonal abilities, and advantage perception from one-of-a-type perspectives. Group treatment can be a treasured possibility for human beings to gain comments, assist, and encouragement from friends who may be going via similar struggles.

3. Skills Training:

DBT abilties training is often executed in a based totally organisation layout. It makes a speciality of training human beings precise skills to control their emotions, navigate hard conditions, and construct more healthy relationships. Skills training usually covers 4 principal modules: mindfulness, distress tolerance, emotion law, and interpersonal effectiveness. Participants research practical strategies and techniques thru psychoeducation, discussions, position-plays, and homework assignments. The aim is to equip people with the important device to deal with distressing emotions, tolerate difficult conditions, adjust their feelings, and decorate their interactions with others.

Overall, DBT can be implemented in diverse settings to help people enhance their emotional well-being, increase powerful coping capabilities, and assemble more wholesome relationships. Whether it's through man or woman remedy, organization treatment, or capabilities schooling, DBT offers a whole technique to resource human beings in their adventure towards emotional stability and a greater pleasant existence.

DBT In Schools Empowers:

Dialectical Behavior Therapy in faculties and academic settings is a recovery approach that allows university college students increase important abilities to govern their emotions, address pressure, and beautify their interpersonal relationships.

In smooth phrases, DBT in faculties lets in university students learn how to take note of the prevailing 2nd, deal with tough conditions without making them worse, recognize and manipulate their feelings, and correctly communicate with others. It provides practical equipment and strategies that may be carried out in numerous conditions, each out of doors and in the study room. By incorporating DBT into schools and academic settings, college college students can beautify their emotional well-being, cope better with academic and private disturbing situations, and construct healthier relationships with their peers and teachers. It creates a supportive and nurturing environment that fosters non-public boom and academic fulfillment.

Overall, DBT in schools empowers college students with the capabilities they want to navigate the usaand downs of lifestyles, equipping them with treasured gear for a brighter future.

DBT Challenges & Adaptations For Kids, Teens, Adults And Individuals With Mental Health Conditions:

Dialectical Behavior Therapy (DBT) has confirmed to be powerful in addressing numerous highbrow health conditions and running with super populations. When making use of DBT with particular populations, which include children, teens, adults, and people with specific intellectual health problems, there are particular traumatic conditions and variations that want to be considered. Let's discover those demanding situations and versions for each population:

1. Children:

Challenges:

Children also can have limited emotional and cognitive development, making it tough for them to understand complex concepts and techniques. They may additionally additionally battle with expressing their emotions and function problem focusing on remedy commands.

Adaptations:

DBT for children typically includes simplifying ideas and using age-appropriate language. Techniques like play treatment and cutting-edge sports activities can be protected to have interaction them correctly. Involving mother and father or caregivers is essential to provide normal manual and assist discovered out abilities.

2. Teenagers:

Challenges:

Teenagers often face specific emotional and social worrying situations, which incorporates identification formation, peer pressure, and educational stress. They can be proof in opposition to treatment, have limited emotional law skills, and conflict with impulsive behaviors.

Adaptations:

DBT for teens focuses on addressing their specific disturbing conditions even as incorporating elements in their every day lives. Therapists want to installation a strong rapport, create a non-judgmental environment, and emphasize the relevance of DBT competencies in their daily lives. Group treatment with friends can be powerful in decreasing feelings of isolation and fostering help.

three. Adults:

Challenges:

Adults may additionally additionally have ingrained sorts of behavior and lengthy-standing emotional problems that require in depth intervention. They also can additionally have trouble prioritizing remedy amidst their obligations and may be proof against exchange.

Adaptations:

Individual treatment is commonly the primary mode of remedy for adults. Therapists may moreover attention on figuring out and enhancing deeply ingrained patterns and beliefs. Incorporating mindfulness practices and validating the individual's studies additionally may be useful. Addressing the sensible limitations to attending treatment, which includes scheduling and transportation, is crucial.

four. Individuals With Specific Mental Health Disorders:

Challenges:

Different intellectual health issues gift specific worrying situations. For instance, individuals with depression may also war with motivation, while humans with tension may additionally experience problems in tolerating distressing conditions.

Adaptations:

Tailoring DBT to precise mental health issues includes knowledge the unique disturbing situations related to every scenario. Therapists may also moreover furthermore prioritize advantageous DBT capabilities based totally really at the character's desires. For instance, emotion law capabilities can be emphasised for people with despair, on the identical time as misery tolerance abilities can be extra relevant for human beings with anxiety. Collaborating with other professionals worried inside the person's care, which consist of psychiatrists or medical docs, can offer a whole treatment technique.

In summary, utilizing DBT to extraordinary populations calls for variations to cope with the particular demanding situations they face. These variations incorporate simplifying concepts, using age-appropriate language, incorporating applicable factors of their each day lives, putting in rapport, concerning caregivers or parents, addressing realistic obstacles, and tailoring the treatment to precise highbrow fitness issues. By thinking about those factors, DBT may be correctly applied to severa populations, supporting them enlarge important abilties for emotional regulation and superior well-being.

DBT For Other Health Disorders:

There are exceptional health issues which can be thorough dealt with with DBT. They are majorly;

Substance Use Disorders (SUD)

Eating issues

Trauma and PTSD

1. DBT For Substance Use Disorders:

DBT is an powerful method used to help human beings struggling with Substance Use Disorders (SUD). SUD refers to the dangerous use of substances like pills or alcohol. DBT for SUD combines elements of cognitive-behavioral remedy and mindfulness strategies to address the underlying issues contributing to substance abuse. In DBT for SUD, human beings have a look at capabilities to manipulate cravings, address pressure, regulate their emotions, and decorate their relationships. The therapy makes a speciality of improving self-interest, reputation of feelings with out judgment, and growing healthy coping mechanisms.

DBT for SUD entails both individual treatment and organization intervals. During individual remedy, the individual works with a therapist to set desires, find out triggers for substance use, and develop techniques to avoid relapse. Group durations offer a supportive environment wherein individuals can percent reports, studies from others, and workout their talents.

The very last purpose of DBT for SUD is to help human beings enlarge a lifestyles nicely properly well worth residing without counting on substances. By studying more healthy strategies to govern feelings, cope with distress, and construct powerful relationships, people can paintings within the path of healing and a satisfying life loose from substance abuse.

2. DBT for Eating Disorders:

DBT is a type of remedy that has verified to be effective in treating consuming issues. Eating problems like anorexia nervosa, bulimia nervosa, and binge consuming sickness can be hard to overcome, but DBT offers a useful technique. DBT in ingesting ailment treatment specializes in helping people enlarge wholesome coping mechanisms and emotional regulation abilties. It goals to deal with the underlying emotional difficulties and belief styles that contribute to disordered ingesting behaviors. DBT also includes mindfulness techniques, which help people emerge as extra aware of their thoughts, feelings, and bodily sensations. This attention allows them to make aware alternatives about their behaviors and expand a more balanced relationship with meals and their our our bodies.

Overall, DBT in eating illness remedy offers a entire and compassionate technique, presenting practical techniques to sell extended-time period recovery and a greater healthful courting with food and oneself.

three. DBT For Trauma & PTSD:

DBT is a restoration method that may be useful for human beings who've experienced trauma or have positioned up-annoying strain infection (PTSD). It pursuits to help people increase abilties to manipulate intense emotions, deal with distressing situations, and enhance relationships.

DBT for trauma and PTSD consists of severa components. One vital aspect is learning mindfulness strategies to increase popularity of the winning second and reduce reactivity to worrying recollections. It moreover emphasizes emotional regulation talents to help people grow to be privy to and control overwhelming emotions that often accompany trauma.

Another issue is growing effective interpersonal capabilities, which can be tough for humans with trauma or PTSD. DBT permits human beings have a look at conversation techniques and strategies to construct healthy relationships on the same time as placing suitable limitations.

Lastly, the treatment makes a speciality of developing misery tolerance capabilities to assist people address triggering conditions or memories. This consists of studying strategies to soothe oneself and tolerate distress without resorting to bad coping mechanisms.

Overall, DBT for trauma and PTSD provides realistic equipment to control signs and symptoms, assemble resilience, and beautify everyday well-being. It is a whole technique that combines elements of mindfulness, emotion law, interpersonal effectiveness, and misery tolerance to manual people on their healing journey.

Application Of DBT in Real-Life Scenarios

Case Study 1: Individual Therapy

Scenario:

Jane is a 35-twelve months-vintage woman who has been identified with borderline character disorder (BPD). She struggles with severe temper swings, self-terrible behavior, and problem retaining strong relationships. Her therapist makes a selection to put in force Dialectical Behavior Therapy (DBT) to help her manipulate her emotions and extend extra healthy coping techniques.

Application Of DBT:

In person treatment classes, Jane works cautiously together along side her therapist to apprehend triggers that purpose emotional dysregulation. They discover past critiques and varieties of conduct, assisting Jane recognize the underlying motives of her struggles. Jane learns mindfulness strategies to turn out to be privy to her thoughts and emotions within the present 2nd. She additionally practices distress tolerance talents, along side the use of self-soothing techniques or carrying out excellent distractions even as confronted with distressing situations.

Through DBT, Jane often learns to modify her feelings and have interaction in more adaptive behaviors. Over time, she develops greater healthy communication patterns, builds resilience, and improves her ability to hold stable relationships.

Case Study 2: Group Therapy

Scenario:

Alex is a 27-365 days-antique college student who struggles with social anxiety disorder. He well-knownshows it hard to have interaction in social conditions and frequently avoids social interactions, which negatively affects his academic and private life. To cope with his social anxiety, Alex's therapist recommends DBT company remedy.

Application Of DBT:

In a DBT agency treatment setting, Alex joins a small institution of those who additionally revel in social tension. Led by using a professional therapist, the employer durations offer a supportive environment wherein individuals can share their stressful situations and studies from each other's tales.

During the organization training, Alex practices interpersonal effectiveness skills, at the facet of assertiveness and active listening, via feature-plays and actual-life situations. He furthermore gets validation and remarks from each the therapist and fellow business enterprise people, which allows him construct self notion and self-esteem. The corporation dynamics provide opportunities for social engagement, allowing Alex to little by little confront his fears and practice new abilties in a secure surroundings. As the group progresses, Alex's social anxiety signs and symptoms decrease, and he income a revel in of belonging and reference to others. He develops a manual network and learns techniques to navigate social conditions extra effectively.

Case Study three: Skills Training

Scenario:

John is a 40-12 months-vintage guy with anger control troubles. He frequently will become enraged in response to minor frustrations, essential to conflicts at paintings and strained relationships along with his family. His therapist introduces DBT abilities training to assist him control his anger and enhance his emotional law.

Application Of DBT:

John participates in DBT competencies schooling training in which he learns specific techniques to control his anger. He practices emotion regulation skills, which encompass identifying and labeling his emotions, and utilizing misery tolerance skills to save you impulsive reactions.

During abilties schooling, John learns interpersonal effectiveness techniques, which interest on effective communication and problem-fixing. Through feature-plays and guided physical video games, he acquires talents to particular his desires assertively and negotiate conflicts in a extra first-class way. As John applies the abilties he learns in therapy to his each day life, he starts to be conscious big improvements. He turns into extra self-conscious and can select out triggers for his anger. John develops greater healthful coping mechanisms and learns to reply to conditions in a calmer and more rational way, main to greater awesome relationships and decreased conflict.

These case studies spotlight the practical software of DBT in extraordinary eventualities, demonstrating how it is able to effectively cope with diverse intellectual health traumatic conditions through presenting people with equipment and strategies to control their emotions, develop interpersonal abilties, and promote everyday properly-being.

Treatment Process Of DBT Application:

The treatment gadget of humans making use of Dialectical Behavior Therapy (DBT) includes numerous steps, which incorporates evaluation, treatment planning, and improvement monitoring. Here is a simplified clarification of every degree:

1. Assessment:

In the assessment phase, the therapist gathers data approximately the man or woman's highbrow health troubles, existence reviews, and contemporary functioning. They can also furthermore behavior interviews, questionnaires, and assessments to advantage a complete knowledge of the character's emotional struggles, behaviors, and interpersonal issues. This assessment permits understand the unique regions that need to be addressed through DBT.

2. Treatment Planning:

Once the assessment is complete, the therapist collaborates with the character to extend a treatment plan tailor-made to their needs. The treatment plan outlines the dreams and objectives of remedy, thinking about the character's particular worrying conditions and strengths. It identifies specific regions to art work on, which incorporates emotion regulation, distress tolerance, interpersonal effectiveness, or mindfulness. The therapist and man or woman communicate the frequency and duration of therapy instructions and installation a hooked up framework for the remedy way.

three. Progress Monitoring:

Throughout the direction of treatment, improvement monitoring is vital to music the character's development and make any vital modifications to the treatment plan. The therapist often assesses the person's improvement in reaching the agreed-upon desires. This may incorporate reviewing finished homework assignments, tracking modifications in symptoms and behaviors, and gathering remarks from the person about their studies. Progress monitoring enables both the therapist and the individual look at the effectiveness of the treatment and make any adjustments required to ensure persevered growth.

In summary, the treatment method of DBT involves assessing the character's troubles and strengths, collaboratively growing a treatment plan, and tracking development over the years. This established technique allows guide therapy training and allows humans to art work within the path of their dreams, acquire new capabilities, and make high-quality modifications of their emotional nicely-being and relationships.

DBT Treatment Journeys:

DBT treatment trips may have each a achievement results and challenges alongside the way. Here is a simplified dialogue of those additives:

Successful Outcomes:

1. Improved Emotional Regulation:

One of the primary goals of DBT is to assist humans extend talents to alter their feelings efficaciously. A a success outcome of remedy is while people discover ways to choose out and manipulate their emotions in healthier techniques. They grow to be higher geared up to address distressing conditions, decreasing impulsive or self-negative behaviors.

2. Enhanced Interpersonal Skills:

DBT specializes in enhancing interpersonal effectiveness, assisting people increase greater healthful relationships. Successful effects encompass people reading assertiveness, energetic listening, and war choice skills. They emerge as greater effective in expressing their needs, putting obstacles, and navigating social interactions efficaciously.

3. Increased Mindfulness:

DBT includes mindfulness strategies to assist humans cultivate recognition in their thoughts, emotions, and physical sensations in the gift second. A a fulfillment very last results is on the identical time as people learn how to workout mindfulness often and enjoy the advantages of prolonged self-interest, reduced reactivity, and improved normal nicely-being.

4. Reduction In Self-Harm and Suicidal Behaviors:

People with BPD regularly warfare with self-harming behaviors and suicidal thoughts. DBT consists of unique strategies to cope with the ones issues, which include distraction techniques, catastrophe survival strategies, and the development of a safety plan. Through the ones interventions, human beings can enjoy a sizable lower in self-adverse behaviors.

Challenges:

1. Resistance To Change:

Some people might also first of all resist effective factors of DBT treatment, particularly while confronting uncomfortable feelings or tough prolonged-held beliefs. Overcoming resistance may be a task, as it calls for building take into account and offering everyday help to encourage individuals to interact virtually inside the therapy gadget.

2. Skill Generalization:

Applying the competencies found in therapy to real-life conditions can be tough. Individuals may additionally war to enforce newly acquired competencies continuously outdoor the remedy putting. It frequently requires ongoing exercising, reinforcement, and guide to effectively generalize abilties and lead them to a herbal part of day by day existence.

3. Relapse and Setbacks:

While development is expected in the course of the remedy journey, setbacks or relapses can rise up. Individuals may additionally experience moments of reverting to vintage styles of conduct or going through new demanding situations that take a look at their acquired skills. Addressing relapses and setbacks calls for resilience, ongoing treatment resource, and the implementation of greater strategies to preserve development.

4. Treatment Duration:

DBT is generally an in depth and prolonged-term remedy. It consists of a determination of numerous months or maybe years, counting on the individual's wishes. The length may be a challenge for folks that are looking for quick solutions or who face obstacles which includes economic constraints or constrained get right of entry to to specialised agencies.

In precis, a achievement outcomes of DBT treatment encompass advanced emotional regulation, higher interpersonal competencies, and prolonged mindfulness. However, demanding situations inclusive of resistance to change, skills generalization, and potential relapses or setbacks can upward thrust up all through the remedy journey. These worrying situations spotlight the significance of ongoing useful resource, staying energy, and endurance in supporting individuals overcome boundaries and benefit lengthy-term brilliant consequences.

It's crucial to be conscious that at the same time as DBT has tested huge effectiveness, really everyone's treatment adventure is particular. The annoying situations confronted may additionally vary from individual to man or woman, and the a success consequences depend upon character dedication, useful resource, and the expertise of the therapist. With perseverance and the right property, many people can advantage excessive fantastic modifications and an advanced first-rate of life thru DBT.

Integrating DBT with Other Treatment Modalities

Dialectical Behavior Therapy (DBT) can be correctly protected with amazing treatment modalities to offer entire address people. Here's a simplified steerage on integrating DBT with distinct methods like medicine manipulate or different recovery techniques:

1. Collaboration And Communication:

Effective integration starts with open conversation and collaboration some of the treatment agency contributors. This consists of therapists, psychiatrists, and specific healthcare specialists worried in the character's care. Regular conferences and facts sharing assist ensure a cohesive treatment plan.

2. Assess Individual Needs:

Assess the individual's precise dreams and decide how specific remedy modalities can complement each different. For instance, examine whether or not or now not medication management is crucial to deal with underlying psychiatric conditions or symptoms that would beat back development in remedy.

three. Coordinate Treatment Goals:

Ensure that the treatment desires at some point of unique modalities align with each exclusive and the character's regular nicely-being. Establish shared goals and paintings together to address the man or woman's intellectual health, emotional regulation, and conduct change needs.

four. Timing And Sequencing:

Determine the most appropriate timing and sequencing of interventions. For example, if medicinal drug is part of the treatment plan, it is probably beneficial to stabilize the person's symptoms and signs first of all through treatment control in advance than delving into extensive DBT talents training.

5. Complementing Approaches:

DBT may be combined with severa restoration modalities, collectively with Cognitive Behavioral Therapy (CBT), Acceptance and Commitment Therapy (ACT), or psychodynamic treatment. Identify how those techniques can supplement each outstanding to deal with particular additives of the character's scenario.

6. Consistency And Continuity:

Ensure consistency and continuity of care via using the usage of often reviewing the treatment plan, comparing progress, and adjusting interventions as wanted. Encourage verbal exchange the diverse treatment group to keep a holistic method and save you conflicting hints.

Chapter 14: Advanced Techniques In Dbt

Let's explore a few advanced thoughts and strategies internal Dialectical Behavior Therapy (DBT) which includes;

Chain evaluation

Validation techniques

Working with co-taking location troubles.

1. Chain Analysis:

Chain evaluation is a center thing of DBT and is used to apprehend and cope with tricky behaviors. It entails breaking down a sequence of sports activities, thoughts, and emotions that bring about a particular behavior. The motive is to find out the triggers, vulnerabilities, and outcomes that maintain the conduct. By analyzing the chain, people can advantage notion into the underlying elements contributing to their movements and broaden opportunity, greater healthy responses.

For example, if someone with self-harming behaviors desires to deal with and alternate this pattern, they may artwork with a therapist to have a have a observe the chain of events that added approximately self-damage. This may additionally moreover contain identifying triggers (e.G., feeling overwhelmed), vulnerabilities (e.G., low misery tolerance), automatic mind (e.G., "I can't cope with this"), and emotions (e.G., anger, disappointment). Through the chain analysis tool, opportunity coping techniques may be advanced to interrupt the dangerous conduct sample.

2. Validation Strategies:

Validation is a vital issue of DBT that entails acknowledging and accepting an individual's thoughts, feelings, and reviews as valid and understandable. It is critical for growing a recuperation surroundings wherein people experience heard and understood, that could decorate their motivation to change. Advanced validation strategies in DBT cross past easy acknowledgement and contain validating each the valid and invalid additives of someone's stories.

In DBT, there are three primary ranges of validation:

a. Accurate Reflection:

This degree entails effectively reflecting the individual's thoughts and emotions without judgment or assessment. It demonstrates that their research are recognized and heard.

b. Normalizing:

This degree includes acknowledging and normalizing the person's reports with the useful aid of highlighting the commonality of their thoughts and feelings in similar conditions. It lets in reduce emotions of isolation or being "peculiar."

c. Radical Genuineness:

This degree involves conveying a deep facts and empathy via absolutely connecting with the person's emotional revel in. It is going past highbrow validation and specializes in growing an proper emotional connection.

By using validation techniques, therapists can assist people revel in understood and massive, developing a foundation for alternate and selling emotional law.

three. Working With Co-Occurring Disorders:

Co-taking place problems talk over with the presence of every a intellectual fitness sickness and a substance use disease (SUD). In DBT, running with human beings who've co-happening problems consists of addressing each conditions concurrently.

Therapists might also moreover hire the subsequent techniques:

a. Integrated Treatment:

DBT can be tailor-made to cope with the proper wishes of human beings with co-happening troubles. It entails integrating techniques from each DBT and substance abuse remedy techniques to provide a complete treatment plan.

b. Targeting Behavioral Patterns:

Therapists help human beings choose out the useful courting among their highbrow fitness symptoms, substance use, and one in every of a type complicated behaviors. Chain assessment is used to understand the triggers and effects of substance use, in addition to the impact of intellectual fitness signs and symptoms and signs and symptoms on substance use.

c. Skills Training:

In addition to teaching emotion regulation, misery tolerance, interpersonal effectiveness, and mindfulness capabilities, therapists can also recognition on abilities particular to substance use and relapse prevention. This can encompass strategies to govern cravings, cope with urges, and enlarge opportunity worthwhile sports.

By addressing co-taking vicinity problems inside the DBT framework, humans accumulate complete remedy that goals every intellectual health and substance use issues, growing the opportunities of successful recuperation. These advanced concepts and strategies interior DBT, together with chain assessment, validation techniques, and working with co-taking place issues, provide humans with valuable system to understand, manipulate, and triumph over their worrying conditions efficaciously.

Current Developments And Research In DBT:

Dialectical Behavior Therapy (DBT) is a shape of psychotherapy which have end up initially superior to deal with borderline character sickness (BPD). Over the years, research and traits in DBT have prolonged its programs to amazing highbrow health situations as nicely. Here are some contemporary upgrades in DBT:

1. Enhanced Adaptations:

Researchers were walking on adapting DBT for various populations and settings. They have advanced superior variations of DBT for teens, individuals with substance use problems, ingesting troubles, and located up-worrying stress disease (PTSD). These adaptations comprise tailoring the remedy to meet the particular goals of these populations, making DBT greater to be had and effective.

2. Technology-Assisted DBT:

The integration of generation into DBT has confirmed promising consequences. Mobile packages and on line structures were advanced to supply DBT skills schooling, mindfulness carrying activities, and track remedy progress. These technological enhancements have the ability to decorate accessibility, fee-effectiveness, and engagement in DBT.

3. Research On Effectiveness:

Numerous studies have investigated the effectiveness of DBT in treating diverse intellectual fitness conditions. Research has constantly shown powerful consequences for DBT in lowering suicidal behaviors, self-damage, and emotional dysregulation in people with BPD. Additionally, DBT has validated effectiveness in treating substance use troubles, consuming issues, depression, tension, and PTSD.

four. Mechanisms Of Change:

Researchers are exploring the underlying mechanisms thru which DBT brings about high-quality change. Neuroimaging studies have provided insights into the neural strategies concerned in emotional law and mindfulness, losing mild on the mechanisms via which DBT works. This knowledge can result in similarly upgrades in treatment and the development of centered interventions.

five. Dismantling And Component Studies:

To better recognize the precise elements of DBT that make a contribution to its effectiveness, researchers have executed dismantling and issue studies. These research incorporate studying the character components of DBT, which includes mindfulness, misery tolerance, emotion law, and interpersonal effectiveness. By figuring out the essential elements, researchers can refine and tailor DBT to maximize its benefits.

6. Implementation And Dissemination:

Efforts are being made to increase the dissemination and implementation of DBT in severa healthcare settings. Training packages and certification techniques for clinicians had been advanced to make certain constancy to the remedy model. Additionally, studies is being done at the implementation of DBT in one-of-a-kind cultural contexts and healthcare structures.

Overall, latest studies and dispositions in DBT have increased its applications, greater its effectiveness, and superior accessibility.

These improvements have the functionality to undoubtedly effect the lives of people with a big variety of highbrow health conditions, supplying them with powerful tools to control their emotions, enhance interpersonal relationships, and lead pleasant lives.

184

www.ingramcontent.com/pod-product-compliance
Lightning Source LLC
Chambersburg PA
CBHW051726020426
42333CB00014B/1169

www.ingramcontent.com/pod-product-compliance
Lightning Source LLC
Chambersburg PA
CBHW051726020426
42333CB00014B/1169